D1519933

C. Wesley

The Music and Hymnody

OF

The Methodist Hymnal

BY

CARL F. PRICE

NEW YORK: EATON & MAINS
CINCINNATI: JENNINGS & GRAHAM

To

My Father

3

CONTENTS

LIST OF ILLUSTRATIONS

PREFACE

To present a dictionary of hymnology, or even to collect critical notes upon all of the seven hundred hymns in the Methodist Hymnal, is not the purpose of this little book: for it would be impossible to do this adequately within the limits of space imposed upon our study; and, besides, the more detailed treatment of the hymns (though not of the tunes) has already been ably presented by other hymnologists of the Church. But as there has often been expressed the need of a brief introduction to the Hymnal, its history, its hymns and tunes, its theology, its musical and literary beauties, together with helpful suggestions to pastors and prayer-meeting leaders—in a word, a practical guide to the Hymnal—this has, therefore, been attempted by the author. Whatever imperfections may mar the work, it is the devout hope of the author that this study may be of some service to the Master's cause in stimulating a deeper interest in the meaning and use of the hymns and tunes.

Hymn-stories are told herein, some of them drawn from the common reservoirs of hymnology, a few recited in these pages for the first time, but for the purpose more of suggesting typical conditions under which hymns are written or sung or quoted, than of explaining particular hymns.

We beg the indulˉence of the Gentle Reader if the

discussion become somewhat technical in a few passages, such as those addressed especially to the versifier, or the musical theorist, or the professional hymnal editor; for each of these classes may find in the Hymnal much material especially worthy of their study.

Our acknowledgments are due to many friends, who have given to us valuable assistance; to the sainted Bishop Goodsell, Chairman of the Hymnal Commission, who during winter evenings, most delightful and precious in memory, explained to the author many of the beauties of the Hymnal; to Professor C. T. Winchester and to Professor Karl P. Harrington for the story of the preparation of the Hymnal; to Mr. Frederick Schlieder for criticism on the musical sections of the book; to Dr. Charles M. Stuart and Dr. W. F. Tillett, editors of the Hymnal, and to Professor Peter C. Lutkin for helpful letters; to Mr. Dewitt Miller, the owner of the Cardinal Newman manuscript, for permission to use it as an illustration; to Mr. A. S. Newman, whose remarkable hymnological library has been of great assistance; to the Methodist Historical Library, where helpful material was placed at our disposal; and to those composers and hymn-writers, whose stories are told for the first time in these pages. *The Christian Advocate* and the *Epworth Herald* we also thank for permission to reprint articles upon hymnology by the author, which first appeared in those periodicals.

CARL F. PRICE.

New York City, June 1, 1911.

INTRODUCTION

IN the presence of music the meditative soul contemplates a mystery. Music wields powers employed by no other art; for the musical art alone can stir the emotions without depicting objects or episodes such as the representative arts demand as a vehicle for expression. Music speaks directly to the heart. It is the language of the emotions. And perhaps it is because God sometimes speaks directly to the heart of man that the poets have called music "the Divine Art." But all art is in a sense sacred, and perhaps Carlyle best describes the attributes of music when he declares:

"Music is a kind of inarticulate, unfathomable speech, which leads us to the edge of the infinite and impels us for a moment to gaze into it."

Whether or not music possesses a divine quality unshared by the other arts, music has become the most helpful of all the arts in the worship of the Divine Father. Said Michael Prætorius: "Music, in the opinion of many, ranks second only to faith and religion." And said Chateaubriand: "Music is the child of prayer, the companion of religion." With what reverence music was esteemed in the Protestant Reformation may be understood from these words of Martin Luther:

"Next to theology I give to music the highest place and honor.

9

"Music is the art of the prophets—the only art that can calm the agitations of the soul: it is one of the most magnificent and delightful presents God has given us."

In quite another sense hymn-writing may be regarded as a Divine Art, since its theme is divinity itself—since its noblest forms demand nothing short of the highest art. The hymn of praise is almost as ancient as divine worship. Each successive age has employed the hymn for an expression of the most intense spiritual emotion. Moses, the law-giver and God-inspired leader of his people, crowned his wonderful career of achievement with a hymn of praise to Him, who made possible all of Israel's victories. David, the shepherd, the harpist, the great executive and king, the brilliant military general, gave vent to the titanic emotions of his spirit in the most wonderful body of hymns ever written—the Psalms. The Virgin Mary, to whom the angel had whispered the sweetest secret since the world began, proclaimed the exalted joy of her soul in the *Magnificat*. The stories of these and other ancient Hebrew hymns are but counterparts of the stories of modern hymns; for out of life have been wrought the best hymns, out of sorrow and soul-conquest, out of joy and revelation. And it is the element of the human soul needs, common to all ages, common to all conditions of men, and the all-sufficiency of God to meet every last, deepest need of the soul, that has enabled a hundred generations of men to appropriate these ancient hymns as their own expression of faith and worship.

Thus the greatest hymns come to be used by all ages. The psalms of Israel's camp-fires and the hymn of the Apostles at the Last Supper blend in thought and emotion with the hymns of these later centuries in one grand Hymn of the Race to

"Our Maker, Defender, Redeemer and Friend."

When these two divine arts are united—music and hymn-writing—each divine in its own peculiar sense, worship finds its noblest expression, prayer its most beautiful form, and praise its loftiest utterance. In view of the peculiarly sacred office of the singing of hymns, it were sacrilege to employ them either with flippancy or indifference. Indeed, to meditate devoutly upon the hymns and their music, to study their meaning and message, and to comprehend the purpose of hymn-singing is to intensify one's reverence for music and hymnody.

Melancthon, once passing along the street at Weimar with his friends in banishment, heard a little girl singing in clear, sweet tones the great hymn of their beloved leader, Luther:

"A mighty fortress is our God,"

and at once he exclaimed, "Sing on, little maid; for you little know what hearts you are comforting." The Church of God knows not what hearts are being cheered, what faith is being stimulated, what souls are being saved by the singing of the sacred hymns of the ages. Those to whom hymn-singing becomes merely perfunctory are apt to forget what a potent influence hymns exert upon life, and the motives that control human action. That life which expresses itself only in hymn-singing is to be despised. But the life that seeks nobility of achievement often finds its most helpful inspiration in Christian hymns, that sing their truths into the heart of mankind and reëcho the divine love-songs of the Eternal Lover of the Soul.

PART I

THE HYMNAL

COLLECTION

OF

PSALMS

AND

HYMNS.

CHARLES-TOWN,
Printed by LEWIS TIMOTHY. 1737.

Title-page of John Wesley's First Hymn Book, said to be not only the First Hymn Book published in America, but "the First Hymn Book compiled for use in the Church of England"

CHAPTER I

THE GENEALOGY OF THE METHODIST HYMNAL

Early Wesleyan Hymnals—Successive Hymnals of the
Methodist Episcopal Church and the Methodist
Episcopal Church, South

In the light of subsequent ecclesiastical events, it is
of peculiar significance to American Methodists that
the first hymnal ever published for use in the Church
of England was prepared by John Wesley in 1736, and
was first printed in 1737 in Charlestown, Georgia.
John Wesley was then a foreign missionary from England to the distant shores of Georgia. Two striking
characteristics of his wonderful career were early dis-
played in the making of that hymnal; his high hymnodic interest and ability, and his remarkable capacity
for work, in that he was able to add to the exacting
duties of an active foreign missionary the preparation
of a pioneer hymn book.

Only two copies of this hymnal are now known to
exist. Julian's "Dictionary of Hymnology" errs in
stating that but one copy is known, and that it is in
England; for a copy is now in possession of the Public
Library in New York City. This copy, in a good
state of preservation, bears upon the title-page the
legend: "A Collection of Psalms and Hymns, Charles-
Town, Printed by Lewis Timothy, 1737." The editorship and authorship of the threescore and ten hymns
are not disclosed, though hymnology has clearly

demonstrated this to be Wesley's collection. The first forty hymns are for use on Sunday, the next twenty on Wednesday or Friday, the rest on Saturday.

Not until 1760 was the next important hymnal of the Church of England prepared (by M. Madan), composed chiefly of the hymns of Wesley and Watts. During that time Methodism as an active, successful propaganda had become established, though not yet as a separate organized Church; and everywhere the Wesleyan doctrines were being taught effectively through hymns, as well as through the preaching of the Word. Charles Wesley published over fifty books and pamphlets of hymns during his hymnodic career.

The particular collection, to which all subsequent Wesleyan Methodist hymnals trace their genealogy, that golden book of Wesley's, that has exerted the largest influence upon Methodism everywhere, was the famous Wesley collection of 1780. This book, as we shall see in another chapter, was retained practically intact by the Wesleyan Methodists as a nucleus for their successive hymnals in the nineteenth century, forming the middle one of three parts, into which the collection naturally divided itself. In the present Wesleyan Hymnal its architecture is still to be traced.

One of the most popular Methodist hymnals of the latter part of the eighteenth century in England, though unauthorized by the Wesleys, was the famous "Pocket Hymn Book," compiled, edited, and published by Robert Spence, of York, about 1784. Starting out as a coachman, Spence had come under the influence of Methodist preaching, and not only became

PSALMS and HYMNS
For Sunday.

I.

Pſalm XXXIII.

1 YE holy Souls, in God rejoice,
   Your Maker's Praiſe becomes your Voice:
   Great is your Theme. your Songs be new
  Sing of his Name, his Word, his Ways,
  His Works of Nature and of Grace,
   How wiſe and holy, juſt and true !

2 Juſtice and Truth he ever loves,
  And the whole Earth his Goodneſs proves;
   His Word the heavenly Arches ſpread :
  How wide they ſhine from North to South !
  And by the Spirit of his Mouth
   Were all the Starry Armies made.

3 Thou gatherest the wide-flowing Seas ;
  Thoſe watry Treaſures know their Place
   In the vaſt Store-houſe of the Deep ;
  He ſpake, and gave all Nature Birth ;
  And Fires and Seas and Heaven and Earth
   His everlaſting Orders keep.

4 Let Mortals tremble and adore
  A GOD of ſuch reſiſtleſs Power,
   Nor dare indulge their feeble Rage :
  Vain are your Thoughts and weak your Hands,
  But his eternal Counſel ſtands,
   And rules the World from Age to Age. .
          A 2   IL

Specimen Page of John Wesley's First Hymn Book

converted, but also started on a new business career that developed him into a prominent publisher. John Wesley severely criticized this "bookseller of York" for using so many of the Wesley hymns from the 1780 hymnal without permission. Nevertheless, the book continued to gain wider acceptance.

That same year, 1784, in America, there assembled the famous Christmas Conference in Baltimore, from which the Methodist Episcopal Church dates its formal existence. Bishop Coke, who was appointed by Wesley to the Methodists in America, was an intimate friend of Robert Spence; and it is not surprising, therefore, that the first hymnal introduced into America after the organization of the new Church was a reprint of the York "Pocket Hymn Book" of Robert Spence. Its title both in England and in America was the same: "A Pocket Hymn Book, Designed as a Constant Companion for the Pious. Collected from Various Authors." Its size also was the same, the covers being five and one half by three and one half inches, and the pages being four and one half by two and one half.

The Preface to the American edition states among other paragraphs: "We intend to strike off an impression of twenty or thirty thousand copies, that the general cry from congregations that they cannot purchase Hymn Books will be stopped. The Hymn Books which have been already published among us are truly excellent. The select Hymns, the double collection of Hymns and Psalms, ... and the Redemption Hymns display great spirituality, as well as purity of diction. The large Congregational Hymn Book is admirable, indeed, but it is too expensive for the poor, who have little time and less money. The Pocket Hymn Book, lately sent abroad in these States, is a most valuable performance for those who are deeply spiritual, but is better suited to the European Methodists. . . . All the excellencies of the former publications are, in a great measure, centered in the present, which contains the choicest and most precious of the Hymns that are to be found in the former editions; and at the same time is so portable that you may always carry it with you without the least inconvenience."

An early suggestion of the benevolent arrangement that has prevailed throughout the history of the Methodist Episcopal publishing house, of devoting the profits of the Concern to philanthropy, is seen in this paragraph of the Preface: "We are the more delighted with this design, as no personal advantage is concerned but the public good alone. For, after the necessary expenses of printing and binding are discharged, we shall make it a noble charity, by applying the profits arising therefrom to the heavy debts of our Churches and Colleges. No motive of a sinister nature has therefore influenced us in any degree to publish this excellent Compilation. It has received the approbation of the Conferences."

The churches are begged to purchase "no Hymn Books, but what are signed with the names of your two Bishops"; and, finally, they are exhorted "to sing with the Spirit and with the understanding also: and thus may the high praises of God be sent up from East to West, from North to South; and we shall be happily instrumental in leading the Devotions of Thousands and shall rejoice to join you in Time and Eternity. We are, Dear Brethren, your faithful Pastors in Christ, Thomas Coke, Francis Asbury." This, then, was the first official hymnal of the Methodist Epsicopal Church.

The General Conference of 1800 in appointing Ezekiel Cooper to be superintendent of the book business of the Church, authorized him to publish books or tracts, approved or recommended by the Book Committee. The hymnal then in use, not being protected by copyright, was being published also by another concern. For this and probably other reasons a revision was made, and a new hymnal was published in 1802, bearing practically the same title-page, adding a quotation from Psa. 104. 33, and the legend: "Philadelphia, Printed by Solomon W. Conrad, For Ezekiel Cooper, No. 118 North Fourth Street, near the Methodist Church." The same Preface, as in the preceding hymnal, with slight variations, bears the signatures of Thomas Coke, Francis Asbury, and Richard Whatcoat. The material of the old book is here rearranged and revised, a few hymns added, and "the poetical numbers and measurement of some of the old hymns improved, that, according to the rules of music, they may agree better with the tunes to which they are sung. Also, in place of certain words and sentiments, others are introduced, which appear more proper and harmonious."

In 1808 another book was added to the hymnal. At the General Conference of this year Ezekiel Cooper resigned, after having increased the assets of the Book Concern from $4,000 to $45,000; and John Wilson was elected his successor as editor and book steward, with Daniel Hitt as his assistant. To this Conference Daniel Hitt submitted a collection of manuscripts, which he had prepared evidently in collaboration with Bishop Asbury, as we find such references in Asbury's diary as these: "August 2, 1807: I have hastily marked above two hundred hymns, taken from the congregational hymn book, to add to a new American edition, which, I hope, will be as good as any extant." "August 30. The hymns for collection occupied my mind much." "Nov. 3. Both Daniel Hitt and myself preached. Nov. 4. We were diligently occupied with our projected hymn book. 6. We were engaged with our collection of hymns," etc.

At the same Conference James Evans of New York made a proposal "for publishing a music book as a standard for the use of the Methodist Churches throughout the United States." The Committee of Review reported adversely on the tune book, but in favor of publishing the manuscripts of Daniel Hitt as a separate book bound together with the old book, advising, however, the alteration of some of the hymns. This report was adopted two days later. That this revision did not consume much time is evidenced by the fact that the new Supplement was copyrighted September 28, 1808, joining its destinies with the old book, and forming what came to be known as "The

Double Hymn Book." The title of the Supplement was "A Selection of Hymns, from Various Authors, Designed as a Supplement to the Methodist Pocket Hymn Book, Compiled under the direction of Bishop Asbury and Published by Order of the General Conference." Beneath a quotation from 2 Cor. 3. 16 were the words: "First Edition, New York, Published by John Wilson and Daniel Hitt, For the Methodist Connection in the United States. John C. Totten, Printer, 1808." The reason for the change of the place of publication from Philadelphia to New York was that by vote of the General Conference of 1804 the Book Concern had been moved from Philadelphia, where it had become unwelcome, and of the two cities proposed for its new home New York had prevailed by a majority of two.

The old Pocket Hymn Book contained 320 hymns, the new Supplement 328. The Preface, unsigned in the first edition, but signed in some later editions by Francis Asbury and William McKendree, makes this apology for the Supplement: "Although we esteem our Hymn Book in present use, among the best, yet in the great and glorious increase of our Church it has been thought defective in size." The Supplement passed under the review of a committee from each Annual Conference with approbation. It is curious to note in the back of the Supplement the advertisement of some of the publications of the Book Concern. The Supplement was also published as a separate volume.

In 1821 a new Hymnal, copyrighted October 30,

was "published by N. Bangs and T. Mason for the Methodist Episcopal Church. Abraham Paul, Printer." Its title eliminated the phrase "Pocket Hymn Book" for the first time: "A Collection of Hymns for the Use of the Methodist Episcopal Church, principally from the collection of the Rev. John Wesley, M.A., late fellow of Lincoln College, Oxford." This Hymnal contained 604 hymns, two doxologies, and a scriptural index. The preface, containing a few of the phrases in previous prefaces, explains the relation of this Hymnal to its predecessor: "The greater part of the hymns contained in the former selection are retained in this, and several from Wesley's and Coke's collections, not before published in this country, are added. The principal alterations which have been made consist in restoring those which have been altered, as was believed for the worse, to their original state, as they came from the poetical pen of the Wesleys, for the following hymns were, except a few which have been taken from other authors, composed by the Rev. John and Charles Wesley—names that will ever be held dear and in high estimation by every lover of sacred poetry."

On February 18, 1836, a fire destroyed the building of the Methodist Book Concern on Mulberry Street, New York city, with a loss of $250,000. Many of the plates of the Methodist publications were totally destroyed, including the Hymnal plates. This necessitated a new edition of the book then in use. Dr. Nathan Bangs, the book steward, prepared this new edition, adding a new Supplement.

When in the year 1844 the question of episcopal rights and its special relation to slavery had hopelessly divided the councils of our Church, and it was deemed wise to the Southern Conferences of the Methodist Episcopal Church that they should separate and form a Church of their own, a plan was proposed whereby the separation should be consummated regularly and in order. The regularity of the actual division of Methodism into two bodies was not recognized by the Methodist Episcopal Church, however, until 1876, when the bitterness of the lamentable dispute gave way to the affectionate interchange of fraternal relations between the two great bodies of Methodism in America.

In May, 1846, the Southern Conferences met in Petersburg for the first General Conference of the Methodist Episcopal Church, South, under whose authority the forms of the new Church were perfected. One question which demanded decision was the preparation of a new Hymnal.   This was first brought before the General Conference on May 5 by a resolution signed by William M. Wightman and Thomas O. Summers, which we quote in full, because of its importance as the first officially recorded step toward a Hymnal of the Methodist Episcopal Church, South:

Whereas, It is highly desirable that various changes and improvements should be made in a new edition of the Methodist Hymn Book, to be published under the authority of this General Conference; *therefore,*

Resolved, That a committee of five be appointed to prepare such a work for publication, as soon as possible, giving in every case the name of the author of the hymn, increasing the number of common, long, and short meters, by selecting from the authorized Wesleyan Hymn Book, and other approved sources, and excluding some of the particular meters, which are unsuitable for the ordinary congregational singing, introducing into the body of the Hymn Book any valuable hymns not to be found in the Supplement, and dispensing with the remainder and making such alterations in the method and arrangement of the subjects as they may deem advisable.

Although the resolution was promptly tabled for the time being, it was taken from the table three days later and referred to the committee, which barely escaped being instructed "to report to this Conference within six days what particular meter hymns they propose to exclude"—an almost impossible task for a hymnal commission in the midst of the excitement and work of so constructive a General Conference as this was. The following day, May 9, it was voted by the Conference that the "Committee on Revision and Publication of our Hymn Book be not required to report to this Conference, but that they be authorized to proceed, as soon as may be," to prepare the Hymnal and have it published. On May 23, shortly before the adjournment was taken, the Bishop appointed as a Committee on the Hymn Book, Thomas O. Summers, William M. Wightman, Jefferson Hamilton, Whiteford Smith, and Augustus B. Longstreet. The Hymnal which they published was in constant use by the Church until 1886. Efforts were made from time to time to modify or supplant the book. At the General Conference of 1858 a resolution and a memorial asking for a Tune Book were referred to the Committee on Tune Hymn Book, who, with the assent of the General Conference, referred it all to the book agent, book editor, and Book Committee, with instructions to take such steps as were advisable.

On May 24 of the 1870 General Conference in the South the Committee on Books and Periodicals reported in favor of authorizing the general book agent to publish a hymn and tune book, appointing as a committee to compile the book Dr. J. M. Bonnell, Dr. Thomas O. Summers (one of the signers of the original resolution in 1846), and Dr. W. P. Harrison. This book was intended as an abridgment of the official Hymnal for use in the poorer churches. On May 13 it is recorded that Professor McIntosh (composer of one of our hymn tunes) was introduced by the Bishop to the Conference, and led the Conference in singing "beautiful pieces from the new Hymn and Tune Book, published by order of the General Conference of 1870." Again on May 24, 1878, the committee reported against the publication of a new smaller Hymnal because of the possibility of an Ecumenical Methodist Hymn Book. A resolution passed, however, the same day, allowing the book editor, the Book Committee, and one bishop at pleasure to publish a small hymn or song book, suited to revival, prayer, and social meetings.

In 1886 a new Hymnal was authorized to take the place of the old book that had done good service since 1846. The Committee on Hymn Book reported on May 19, referring to a pan-Methodistic Hymnal, but begging "to be excused from further consideration of the subject in the absence of any definite information as to the wishes and purposes of our sister Churches."

On May 22, however, their report as adopted authorized the College of Bishops to appoint a committee of nine, to be divided into three equal sections, as was the Methodist Episcopal Hymnal Committee of 1878. This committee was instructed to prepare a Hymnal under these rules: No hymn to be excluded without a two-thirds vote; no hymn not in the Hymnal to be admitted without a two-thirds vote; the numbers in the indexes shall refer to the hymns. It was recommended that those hymns be excluded which are rarely or never used in public or social worship, that when it can be judiciously done the long hymns be abridged, and that none exceed twenty-four lines; that particular attention be paid to arrangement and classification of hymns according to subjects; that the whole number of hymns do not exceed 800. This Hymnal, first published in April, 1889, was the book which the present Methodist Hymnal supplanted in the South. It contained, besides 842 hymns, a Supplement of seventy-six sacred songs for use in prayer meetings and Sunday schools.

Two years after the Methodist Episcopal Church, South, in their 1846 General Conference had ordered a new Hymnal, the General Conference of the Methodist Episcopal Church, meeting in May, 1848, also decided upon a revision. The movement was officially started by the Rev. Dr. James Floy, who on May 2 moved that a committee of seven be appointed to consider the revisal of the Hymn Book, and report if they deemed improvement necessary. This committee, consisting of C. Elliott, chairman, Matthew Simpson, W. Hosmer,

James Floy, David Patten, G. F. Brown, and Nelson Rounds, reported in favor of the revision, which the Book Committee in New York had joined the official editors in requesting; and the report stipulated that the committee of seven be appointed by the General Conference, that they submit their work for approval to the editors, the Book Committee at New York, and the bishops, and that the expenses of revision be defrayed by the book agents.

One amendment to the report proposed to make a majority of the committee "traveling preachers in the regular pastoral work," and, although it was lost, it voiced a feeling still prevalent, that pastors are good judges of what the Hymnal should be.

A nominating committee of seven was appointed on May 10, and on May 23 reported the following names for the Committee of Revision, who were elected forthwith: David Dilley, Philadelphia Conference; J. B. Alverson, Genesee Conference; James Floy, New York Conference; David Patten, Jr., Providence Conference; F. Merrick, Ohio Conference; Robert A. West, of Brooklyn; David Creamer, Baltimore. This Hymnal was in use for three decades—longer than any other official Hymnal in the history of the Church.

No important effort toward another revision was made until 1872, and even then the effort failed of immediate results; for, while the special committee appointed to consider the question, "Ought the Hymn Book of the Methodist Episcopal Church to be revised?" reported affirmatively, the General Conference did not adopt its report.

Four years later, 1876, a flood of memorials and resolutions forced the question before the General Conference with better success. On May 4, J. N. Brown successfully presented a resolution that a committee of nine be appointed to consider the propriety of revising our Hymn and Tune Books, so as to adapt them more perfectly to general use in all our churches and congregations. The committee, enlarged to twelve, reported on May 19 that a revision was "imperatively demanded," and that the General Conference authorize the Board of Bishops to appoint a committee of fifteen to be divided into three sections for convenience, and to meet as a whole after each section had completed its assigned work. A two-thirds vote was necessary for the admission of new hymns, or the exclusion of old hymns from the book. The work when completed must needs be submitted to the bishops for their approval, and then a tune book be prepared to fit the Hymn Book. This last proved to be a serious embarrassment to the musical editors, as they were obliged to rigidly follow the order fixed for the hymns, so that some hymns had to be sung to tunes in another part of the book. It was expressly stipulated that no compensation beyond expenses was to be paid to the committee. This was the 1878 book which in the North the present Methodist Hymnal supplanted.

A committee of six, the Rev. J. H. Vincent, afterward elected to the episcopacy in 1888, the Rev. J. S. Chadwick, James M'Gee, A. S. Newman, John E. Searles, Jr., and John J. Matthias, was appointed by the General Conference of 1884 to make a hymnal for the Sunday schools, and the excellent "Epworth Hymnal No. 1" was the result.   A proposal for an interdenominational hymnal was laid before the General Conference of 1892, urging the Church to join the Methodist Episcopal Church, South, the Baptists, Presbyterians, and Congregationalists in preparing a book for Sunday schools, young people, prayer meetings, and revivals; but the resolution came to naught. In the General Conference of 1896 several resolutions failed of passage looking to the publication of an abridged edition of the too large Hymnal then in use. But until the movement which resulted in the present Methodist Hymnal no effective measures were taken to supplant or revise the Hymnal of 1878.

CHAPTER II

THE MAKING OF THE HYMNAL

AT the close of the nineteenth century there was a strong feeling that the Methodist Episcopal Church was in need of a new Hymnal. The old Hymnal had been in use for about a quarter of a century, and while it had served the needs of the Church, and had endeared itself to Methodists throughout the country, the need for a change was recognized as imperative. The first expression given to this sentiment was a series of memorials and resolutions brought before the General Conference of 1900 from various sources. The result of this movement was Report No. 12 of the Committee on Book Concern, adopted on May 29 as signed by Hon. Leslie M. Shaw, chairman of the committee, then governor of Iowa, and a delegate to the General Conference from the Upper Iowa Conference:

DEAR FATHERS AND BRETHREN: Your Committee, to whom were referred certain memorials relative to a Church Hymnal, beg leave to submit the following report:

Whereas, The present Hymnal contains a large number of hymns which are rarely, if ever, used, and are therefore unnecessary, and render the book too large and too expensive for common use; and,

Whereas, A large number of our churches, especially in small towns and country charges, do not use our Church Hymnal at all, but in its place a variety of unofficial, independent song books, and which in many cases are pernicious, to the damage of the Church spiritually, and of our publishing interests financially;

Therefore, there is hereby authorized the preparation of a Hymnal of octavo size, of about six hundred hymns, in which there shall be a small percentage of the best modern hymns and spiritual songs, and also the ritual and order of service of the Methodist Episcopal Church, the same to be sold at the lowest practicable cost.

Your Committee further recommends that the Board of Bishops be authorized to appoint a committee of nine to carry out the provisions hereof.

The committee of nine was appointed by the bishops in accordance with the resolution, and a glance at their individual records is a convincing evidence that the bishops chose wisely the makers of the new Hymnal:

The Rev. Dr. Samuel F. Upham, the chairman of the committee, had been a pastor in the Providence and New England Conferences, and in 1881 was elected professor of practical theology in Drew Theological Seminary. His death occurred on October 5, 1904, before the deliberations of the Joint Commission were completed.

The Rev. Dr. W. A. Quayle, then pastor of Saint James Church, Chicago, and afterward (1908) elected bishop, has long been recognized as one of the most eloquent preachers in American Methodism, as well as a writer of purest literary style. He is one of the very few bishops elected to the episcopacy directly from the pastorate.

The Rev. Dr. Charles W. Smith, then editor of the Pittsburg Christian Advocate, was elected bishop by the General Conference of 1908. He had served many pastorates and a presiding eldership in the Pittsburg

Conference previous to his election to the editorship, in 1884.

The Rev. Dr. Charles Macauley Stuart was professor of sacred rhetoric in Garrett Biblical Institute at the time of the revision, after having served as associate editor of the Michigan Christian Advocate and the Northwestern Christian Advocate, of which he is now the editor.

The Rev. Dr. Camden M. Cobern, for many years a pastor in the Erie, Detroit, Colorado, and Rock River Conferences, was elected professor of English Bible and philosophy of religion in Allegheny College, 1906. At the time of the Hymnal revision he was pastor of Trinity Church, Denver.

The Rev. Dr. Richard Joseph Cooke, at that time editor of The Methodist Advocate Journal (Chattanooga, Tenn.), had been active for years as preacher and pastor, and as professor of New Testament exegesis and historical theology, and later as vice-chancellor and acting president of Grant University. The General Conference of 1904 elected him book editor of his Church. He has rendered distinguished service on the Commissions on the Federation of Episcopal Methodism, the Constitution, the Ritual, and the Judiciary Committee.

The Rev. Dr. Charles S. Nutter, then presiding elder of the Saint Albans District of the Vermont Conference, is well known throughout Methodism as the author of "Hymn Studies," and as one of the foremost hymnologists in America.

Caleb T. Winchester, L.H.D., author, lecturer, and

since 1873 professor of English literature in Wesleyan University, has long been regarded in the literary world and among the colleges as a distinguished authority upon English literature.

Matthew V. Simpson, the son of Bishop Simpson, was a business man in Philadelphia.

When the committee held its first meeting in New York there existed some doubt as to what the nature of the new Hymnal should be, the wording of the resolution not being explicit on that important point. One party held that the General Conference had authorized only a prayer-meeting book, such as the Epworth Hymnal of 1884, to be used as an abridged form of the general Hymnal. Another party, and strongly in the majority, insisted that the proposed Hymnal was intended to supplant the Hymnal of 1878, and should, therefore, be treated as a revision of that book. Upon one point all were agreed, and that was that the new Hymnal should be much shorter than the old, consisting of about five or six hundred hymns.

It was toward a revision of the Hymnal that the committee finally agreed to work, and in their subsequent meetings they had made great progress to this end, when suddenly their work was halted. Already they had agreed upon a large proportion of the hymns, and had formulated the general plan of the book. On January 16, 1902, announcement was made that the book would be ready for the press in August, and printed by December. It might be interesting, if safe, to conjecture what manner of Hymnal this first committee would have produced, had their work continued without interruption. Probably the book would have been much shorter than the Hymnal that was finally produced, for their ambition to make a book of only a little more than five hundred hymns could more easily have been attained had they chosen their old hymns from the 1,117 different hymns in the old Methodist Episcopal Hymnal, instead of from two Hymnals, North and South, containing nearly 1,700 different hymns. Then, too, the Hymnal might have had fewer of the American evangelistic type of tunes, which for many years in the Southern Hymnal and its Supplement have been preserved like pressed flowers in an old volume, flowers that are now cherished less for their fragrance than for the memories which they awaken.

The reason for the discontinuance of the first commission was the discovery that the same General Conference (1900) that had authorized them to prepare a new Hymnal, had also authorized "prompt steps being taken for the preparation of a common Catechism, a common hymn book, and a common order of public worship, and that other branches of Methodism be invited to coöperate in this undertaking" (Report of the Committee on Federation, General Conference, 1900).

In the meantime the Methodist Episcopal Church, South, was also preparing for a common Hymnal. Their General Conference met in Dallas, Texas, in May, 1902. Both of the fraternal delegates from the North referred in their speeches to the common Hymnal. The Rev. Dr. Dewitt C. Huntington said: "We read from the same Bible, we are soon to sing from the same book of hymns, and teach our children the same Catechism. We agree in many things. We differ in few. It would seem that the joint heirs to an inheritance so sacred, fellow workers under the same system of Christian doctrine, striving for the same goal—a regenerated world—should be drawn into an ever-deepening fellowship of labor and love." Lieutenant-Governor John L. Bates, afterward governor of Massachusetts, echoed this sentiment in saying that "when steps are taken to prepare a common hymn book and a common order of public worship," and since other significant events have occurred within the quadrennium just closed, "then the day of the benefits of a practical union, whether one in name or not, is near at hand."

On May 22, the fourteenth day of the General Conference, the Rev. Peter H. Whisner, of the Baltimore Conference, moved to suspend the rules and to adopt Report No. 1 of the Committee on Federation. This report breathes the spirit of fraternal regard for the Methodist Episcopal Church, reciprocating the cordial sentiments of its fraternal delegates, and resolves among other things: "That the bishops of our Church are authorized to act in concert with the bishops of the Methodist Episcopal Church in the work of preparing a common Hymnal for public worship, a common Catechism, and a common order of worship, and to proceed as soon as practicable to appoint the committees for the same as agreed upon by the joint commission." This report was signed by the Rev. P. H. Whisner, chairman, and the Rev. J. P. McFerrin.

The conflict of legislation in the General Conference of the Methodist Episcopal Church was referred to the Board of Bishops, and they nullified the appointment of the old commission of nine, at once reappointing the same nine members to the new joint commission, and increasing the representation of the Methodist Episcopal Church to eleven by adding Bishop Daniel A. Goodsell and the Rev. H. G. Jackson. Subsequently, upon the resignation of M. V. Simpson, J. M. Black was appointed in his place.

Bishop Goodsell (1840–1909), as pastor in the New York East Conference from 1859 to 1887, editor of two religious weeklies, and secretary of the Board of Education, achieved the distinction of being one of the most scholarly and brilliant men ever elected to the episcopacy.

The Rev. H. G. Jackson has for years been a prominent Chicago pastor.

Mr. J. M. Black is well known as an editor and composer of gospel songs.

Like their brothers from the North, the Southern commissioners were chosen for special qualifications for the work in hand. Bishop Elijah Embree Hoss, D.D., LL.D., formerly president of Martha Washington College, and later of Emory and Henry College, professor in Vanderbilt University, and editor of the Nashville Christian Advocate, was elected Bishop of the Methodist Episcopal Church, South, in 1902.

The Rev. Dr. George B. Winton has achieved a

versatile record as pastor in California, missionary in Mexico, professor of Latin in Santa Rosa, and author of Spanish and American works.   In 1902 he was elected editor of the Christian Advocate (Nashville, Tenn.).

The Rev. Dr. Horace M. DuBose, pastor of several churches successively in California, Texas, and Mississippi, and once editor of the Pacific Methodist Advocate, was in 1898 elected secretary of the Epworth League and editor of its organ, the Epworth Era.

The Rev. Dr. Wilbur Fisk Tillett, the hymnologist of his Church, and author of many denominational and theological works, has been associated with Vanderbilt University, of which he became in 1886 vice-chancellor and dean of the theological faculty.

The Rev. Dr. Paul Whitehead, now deceased, was a presiding elder in the Virginia Conference.

The Rev. Dr. John Monroe Moore, pastor of various churches in Texas and Missouri, has been managing editor of the Christian Advocate (Nashville) since 1906.

Edwin Mims, Ph.D., author of works on literature, and editor since 1905 of the South Atlantic Quarterly, is professor of English Literature in Trinity College, N. C.

Henry Nelson Snyder, Lit.D., LL.D., after teaching in Vanderbilt University and Wofford College, became president of the latter institution in 1902.

Rev. Dr. F. S. Parker, a member of the Louisiana Conference, is secretary of the Epworth League of his Church, elected in 1908.

Rev. Dr. James Campbell, of the North Texas Conference, was presiding elder of the Corsicana District.

The Rev. Dr. Robert Thomas Kerlin served as professor in Missouri Valley College, Southwestern University, and the State Normal School, Warrensburg, Missouri, and is now instructor in English at Yale University.

The two Churches were fortunate in being represented by such a remarkable group of men, who combined an alert scholarship and insight into the needs of the Church with a devout sense of the deep spiritual importance of their work. Their proceedings recall the spirit in which Professor Calvin S. Harrington entered upon the work of the Hymnal Commission of 1876–78. In the words of his biography, as related by his wife: "He received the appointment as the greatest honor the Church had ever conferred upon him. Not until after days of prayer and questioning of his fitness did he enter tremblingly, but joyfully, upon the important work. As the days went on, and the labors increased, his enthusiasm grew intense, and absorbed every hour that could be spared from his regular college duties."[1]

Work of such far-reaching influence is not "to be entered into unadvisedly, but reverently, discreetly, and in the fear of God"; and the commission felt with deep earnestness the burden of its responsibility. That they must prepare a Hymnal to be acceptable to the largest Protestant body in America, to serve the Church possibly for three decades, like its predecessors,

---

[1] "Calvin Sears Harrington," by his Wife, Middletown, Connecticut, 1885.

to meet the needs of two separate Churches, to satisfy the varied tastes of every section and almost every class of people in our land, to give expression to the larger vision of truth and the more tender conception of God and his ways with men, which the Church had gained within a generation, to utter this expression without offense to those who still cling to the older ideas—this seems to have been the symphony, as Channing would have styled it, which the commission purposed to construct, composing a harmonious whole out of the themes of three hundred saintly singers of the Christian ages, and the melodies of nearly as many composers.

With this purpose in view the committee assembled for its first meeting in Nashville, Tennessee, in the spring of 1903.

The second meeting was held at Plymouth, Massachusetts, during the first week in July, 1903. In all these sessions a devout spirit of industry pervaded the work of the commission, whose brotherly harmony was never once broken, and whose final meeting (in Washington, D. C., January 14, 1904) was a Pentecost, as Bishop Goodsell reminds us in the Preface.

This meeting practically completed the work of choosing the hymns, though there were still a few minor changes to be made. Most of the tunes had been selected at the final meeting in Washington. Those still not chosen were left to the musical editors and the committee on tunes. The minor changes in phraseology were left with the Hymnal editors, the Rev. Dr. Charles M. Stuart, for the North, and the

Rev. Dr. W. F. Tillett for the South, both of whom we have already mentioned. The musical editors were Professor Karl P. Harrington, of Wesleyan University, and Professor Peter C. Lutkin, of Northwestern University.

Professor Harrington is the son of the late Dr. Calvin Sears Harrington, who for many years occupied the chair of Latin at Wesleyan University, now held by his son, only one incumbent having intervened between father and son. Another pleasing coincidence was that Professor Calvin S. Harrington was one of the two musical editors of the 1878 Hymnal. Born in 1881, Professor Karl P. Harrington since his graduation from Wesleyan, 1882, has been a teacher of Latin, University of Maine and University of North Carolina being two of the colleges he has served. He is well known as an organist, musical director, composer, and lecturer.

Professor Lutkin is professor of music in the College of Liberal Arts and dean of the School of Music in Northwestern University. He was born of Danish parents in 1858 at Thompsonville, Wisconsin, near Racine, to which he moved while a young child. At nine years of age he was a choir boy in the Cathedral of Saint Peter and Saint Paul, Chicago, at twelve an assistant organist there, and at fourteen, now orphaned, he was appointed organist of the Cathedral. In 1881 he went to Europe, where he studied under the great masters. He has been on the Northwestern University faculty since 1891.

The injustice of omitting the names of the musical

editors from the first edition of the new Hymnal, as in every edition of the 1878 Hymnal, was remedied in later editions.

The musical editors and the Tune Committee met in Evanston, Illinois, in the summer of 1904 to complete the tunes, but the work was still unfinished. Before the next meeting a pamphlet was published with the words of several hymns, for which the editors invited new music. The results were discussed by correspondence, and final decision was made in the last meeting in Boston, in the spring of 1905. The general editors and musical editors unite in especially commending the work of Professor C. T. Winchester in selecting tunes for the hymns, in addition to the regular work assigned him on the commission.

CHAPTER III

THE COMPLETED HYMNAL OF 1905

The Book and Its Characteristics—Comparison with Other Hymnals—Some Superlatives

THUS, after years of preparation, the Methodist Hymnal was presented to the Church in September, 1905. It was published simultaneously in uniform editions by the publishing agents of the Methodist Episcopal Church, Eaton & Mains, and Jennings & Graham; and also of the Methodist Episcopal Church, South, Smith & Lamar. The book appeared in two forms, the music edition and the word edition. The former was printed in octavo size, from Gilson music plates made in Boston, the hymns being in 8-point type, the Psalter in 10-point type. The word edition was printed in 16mo size, both hymns and Psalter being in 10-point type. These editions were presented in various cloth and leather bindings, bearing on the back and on the cover the legend in gilt letters, "The Methodist Hymnal." The most beautiful copy of the Hymnal, printed on Oxford India paper and bound in red seal-skin, was presented by Bishop Goodsell, on behalf of the Hymnal Commission, to President Theodore Roosevelt, who acknowledged the favor in pleasing terms.

Between the covers of the Hymnal and spread upon the table of its pages, there lies a sumptuous feast of hymns and music, gathered from the fields of many lands and many ages, meat and drink for the nourishment of the spiritual life, stimulation for sin-sick souls, and refreshment for weary workers.

As soon as the book was published widespread comment upon so important a Hymnal was at once begun. Much of this was in the form of strong commendation. The higher standards, literary and musical, upon which the Commission proceeded, were indorsed, as well as their taste in matters theological. But from some quarters the comment assumed the tone of adverse criticism, futile as such criticism must be, in view of the fact that Methodist hymnals are usually revised only once in a generation.

Some of the comments upon the Hymnal illustrated the dangers of irresponsible criticism on church affairs. Many of those who have criticized the book have done so without having acquired any intelligent or intimate familiarity with its contents. At the close of a Sunday morning's service in New England, soon after the Hymnal was published, a critic assailed one of the makers of the Hymnal, declaring that he disliked the new Hymnal. When pressed for a reason the only one that he could give was that Fanny Crosby's hymns were left out of the book. The reply was simple, and revealed the ignorance of the critic. The new Hymnal contains five of her hymns, whereas there were none in the old Methodist Episcopal Hymnal. Still others have centered their criticism upon minor imperfections of the book, made necessary in some respects by the very nature of the book as a compromise. They would carelessly condemn the book without really understanding its value. A few hours of earnest study would reveal to them treasure-wonders of which they had scarcely ever dreamed.

We would not be understood as imputing ignorance to every critic, or to everyone who feels that the Hymnal has not perfectly represented his own tastes. In fact, every member of the Hymnal Commission could probably be included in the latter class, and the writer and perhaps the reader of these lines. The difficulty is that each tends to criticize from an entirely different angle. The great Methodist Churches, forming the largest Protestant body in America, must satisfy in their forms of worship entirely opposite needs and divergent tastes. When it is remembered that this Hymnal must be used by East and West, South and North, rich and poor, the erudite and the less educated, in the metropolis and in the hamlet, it must be regarded as wonderful in its adaptability to Methodism at large.

One of the most frequent criticisms is that the book contains much more English music and not so much American music as the previous books; and this complaint is urged against the book chiefly by the purveyors of modern gospel music. The indictment is true. The contemporary school of English tune-makers has exerted a predominating influence in the new music of this Hymnal; but so they have also in the hymnals of most other denominations, both in England and in America, and their elevating influence upon church music is constantly rising throughout Protestantism, like an irresistible tide. On the other hand, one frequently hears complaints that too many gospel tunes are included in the book. But, when it is considered how few they really are, after all, this criticism seems over-rigorous. To deny entirely the value of the gospel hymns would be to confess one's unfamiliarity with the history of Methodism. It is true that the average musical standard of the Hymnal is somewhat lowered by this class of music. But surely its place in our social worship is sufficiently important to justify including some of the best of these tunes in the Hymnal. The fact still remains that the collection contains hundreds of the very best hymn tunes in existence, and these criticisms are made only upon a smaller part of the whole.

Another favorite diversion of the critic—and in this field his name is legion—is to complain that some old familiar hymn has been set to a different tune from the one to which it was formerly sung. In some instances this point is well taken, but in other cases it is influenced largely by the personal equation of the critic. It would be difficult to get a company of such critics to agree as to which are the old familiar tunes that should have been kept in the book. Doubtless the editors had reason for every divorce of a hymn from its tune. Had not such reasons been applied to successive revisions, we would still be singing some of the impossible tunes of the earlier days. We would not be suiting the needs of modern worship to the higher tastes of later generations. From the personal standpoint, however, it is hard to dissociate a hymn from the tune to which we have sung it since childhood; and it is not surprising that each successive revision has provoked this comment.

In spite of these criticisms the Methodist Hymnal remains as a great collection of the great hymns and tunes of the Church, and as such it is worthy of the loyal appreciation of the Church at large. There are but few members of any General Conference that are entirely satisfied with every clause of the Discipline. But they cheerfully and loyally accept it as the ultimate result of many forces, some of them contending in opposite directions, but all of them together producing a higher wisdom; and under the new Discipline they loyally return to their various fields of labor for another quadrennium of work. Likewise, the Hymnal should be adopted by every Methodist society as the only authorized hymnody and music for our Church.

Perhaps the most exact method of reaching a just estimate of the Hymnal is to compare it with other American hymnals in the same field. In the first place, comparing it with its predecessors in both North and South, the Hymnal is distinctly an advance in musical, literary, and theological standards. Nor could the Church expect anything other than an advance in all of these respects. Besides, by the arrangement of the material, it marks a decided improvement over the former books.

Just how far the editors have culled their material from the old Hymnals of the Methodist Episcopal Church and the Methodist Episcopal Church, South, may be seen from the following statistics:

In the new Hymnal there are 717 hymns (exclusive of the doxologies, chants, and occasional pieces). They are set to 773 tunes, 216 being duplicates and 557 being different tunes.   Of these 773 tunes,

198   in the old Methodist Episcopal Hymnal were sung to the same words as in the new.

140 in   the old Methodist Episcopal Church, South, Hymnal were sung to the same words as in the new.

105   are tunes from the old Methodist Episcopal Hymnal, set to old words, to which other tunes were used in the old book.

132 are   tunes from the Methodist Episcopal Church, South, Hymnal, set to old words, to which other tunes were used in the old book.

45   are tunes from the old Methodist Episcopal Hymnal, to which new hymns have been set.

46 are   tunes from the Methodist Episcopal Church, South, Hymnal, to which new hymns have been set.

213   are tunes not in the old Methodist Episcopal Hymnal, but are set to hymns that were in the old book.

190 are   not in the old Methodist Episcopal Church, South, Hymnal, but are set to hymns that were in the old book.

212   are tunes not in the old Methodist Episcopal Hymnal and are set to words not in the old book.

265 are   tunes not in Methodist Episcopal Church, South, Hymnal, and are set to words not in the old book.

773 773

In each of the old Hymnals there were only seven hymns set to more than one tune; but the new Hymnal contains two tunes for each of fifty-five hymns, besides three tunes for each of the two hymns, J. G. Holland's "There's a song in the air" and Charles Wesley's "Jesus, Lover of my soul."

In the old Methodist Episcopal Hymnal there were 483 tunes (79 being duplicates, leaving 404 different tunes), to which 1,117 hymns were set. In the old Methodist Episcopal Church, South, Hymnal there were 696 tunes (239 being duplicates, leaving 457 different tunes), to which 918 hymns were set. The new Hymnal has decreased the number of hymns (by just 400 from the Methodist Episcopal Hymnal, by 201 from the Hymnal of the Methodist Episcopal Church, South), and has increased the number of different tunes (by 153 over the Methodist Episcopal Hymnal, by 100 over the Hymnal of the South).

In only one instance in the new Hymnal, namely, the two hymns to the tune "America," are two adjacent hymns set to the same tune, although nearly half of the hymns in the Hymnal of the Methodist Episcopal Church, South, and more than half of those in the Methodist Episcopal Hymnal were adjacent to some other hymn set to the same tune. Frequently in both of the old books the words were placed on a page opposite the tune. This does not occur in the new Hymnal. Nor is the congregation in singing any hymn obliged to turn over to some other part of the Hymnal for the music of that hymn, as was true of fifty-two hymns in the old Methodist Episcopal Hymnal, but of only one hymn in the Hymnal of the Methodist Episcopal Church, South. In a word, each tune is printed with its hymn, and each hymn with its tune. This has made it possible in every instance (save in "America," cited above) to insert the first verse of each hymn between the clefs of the music, to which it is to be sung—a distinct gain in this Hymnal over its predecessors.

Comparing the Methodist Hymnal with other American hymnals, no one would claim for this Hymnal that it excels *all* others in the high standard of its music. Undoubtedly other hymnals, especially those of the Protestant Episcopal Church, as the Hutchins, Parker, or Tucker hymnals, maintain throughout a higher average of music. As we have already observed, the musical average has been somewhat lowered by admitting a small number of hymn tunes especially adaptable to evangelistic work. But as most of our tunes coincide with those in the best hymnals, and as many of our new tunes are of a high order, the musical difference is not great. What is best in the best hymnals is to be found in our own, to which has been added a certain desirable adaptability to our own needs, entirely lacking in the other hymnals.

There is no question that in theology our Methodist doctrinal teachings are better set forth in the Methodist Hymnal than in any other American hymnal. In fact, one of the great dangers to our system of religious education lies in the fact that so many unauthorized hymnals are used in the Church that either teach that which we do not regard as Methodist belief, or else portray the Christian life in false colors by means of weak, sentimental phrasing of little literary and less theological value.

The Methodist Hymnal has found a peer in the excellent book of our Methodist brethren in England, known as "The Methodist Hymn Book." To this book, more than to any other in existence, our Hymnal bears a close relation in the fact that both have been historically derived from the original collection of the Wesleys, and in the possibility that eventually both may be merged into one pan-Methodistic hymnal.

The centripetal force, that is more and more uniting all denominations throughout Protestantism, has made itself felt throughout the several branches of Methodism. The Ecumenical Methodist Conference, first convened in London, September, 1881, has been the best expression of this Wesleyan unity. At the third Ecumenical Conference, held in London, September, 1901, a resolution was presented authorizing one common hymnal for international Methodism. This is a step in advance of the Church of England and the Protestant Episcopal Church, which use entirely different hymnals. The idea has strongly appealed to Methodists on both sides of the sea; and in view of the possibility in the future of an international hymnal we feel justified in quoting from the report on the proposed resolution, adopted on September 9, 1901:

The Business Committee regards the suggestion of the resolution with sympathy and trusts that at some future day it will be realized; but, having regard to the fact, first, that several Churches in the Eastern section have recently published new hymn books, and thereby incurred great financial responsibilities; secondly, that arrangements for the publication of a new hymnal by the Methodist Episcopal Church are in an advanced stage; thirdly, that the Wesleyan Methodist Church has decided to publish a new hymn book, which it is hoped will also be adopted by the Irish New Connection, Wesleyan Reform Union, and Australian Methodist Churches, and having regard to the legal and financial difficulties involved in the proposal, the committee is of the opinion that the proposal contained in the resolution is not at present practicable.

Whether or not the time will ever come when we shall be constrained to join hands across the sea in making one hymnal for all English-speaking Methodists, it is of interest for us to know what manner of hymn book is used by British Methodism.

"The Methodist Hymn Book with Tunes" is the official title of the book. The title-page bears the statement that the music has been edited by Sir Frederick Bridge, M.V.O., Mus.Doc., King Edward Professor, University of London, and for years organist of Westminster Abbey. His works are much studied in this country by students of harmony, and he is regarded as one of the foremost musical scholars in Great Britain. Twenty-nine hymn tunes in his book attest his ability as a composer in this simple form.

The Preface contains the genealogy of the English Methodist Hymnal. The last Wesleyan Hymn Book with Supplement had been issued in 1875, and two years later a tune book was published to conform to this hymn book. This was "the first official tune book in the history of British Methodist psalmody, in which hymns and tunes were printed together on the same page," says the Preface to the present edition.

The Wesleyan Conference of 1900 appointed a committee to coöperate with other British Methodist bodies in preparing a new hymn book, "to cover the whole ground of our Wesleyan Methodist worship, doctrine, and experience, and that the substance of Wesley's original hymn book, with certain modificacations, would find its fitting place in the central portion of the book, which deals with the offer of the gospel and the history of Christian experience." In 1901 a new committee, including laymen, was appointed, who carried the work through to a successful completion in 1904, and presented to the Wesleyan Methodist Church, the Methodist New Connection, the Wesleyan Reform Union, and the Methodist Church of Australasia, a common Methodist Hymn Book, uniting them for the first time through the same songs of the religious life.

This English Hymn Book contains 981 hymns, set to 893 different tunes, besides ten ancient hymns and canticles with several musical settings for each, and thirty-nine supplemental tunes in the Appendix, commonly known as "old Methodist tunes." Many of the tunes are not confined to one page. Sir Arthur Sullivan's magnificent anthem setting of Croft's "St. Anne" covers four pages, and his "Lux in Tenebris" two and a half pages, the music for each separate verse being printed in full. For the first tune of "Dies Irae" an ancient plain-song melody is used, covering six pages; to which is added a second tune of a page and a half. Thus upon perusing the book, one is impressed with its ample provisions, filling almost double the number of pages of our own Hymnal, exclusive of the Psalter.

The Wesleyan Church makes use of a much larger body of the Wesley hymns than has the American

Church. Of the three hundred hymns omitted from the old book in England about one hundred were Wesley's; and still one half of the new Hymn Book consists of hymns by Charles Wesley (437) and John Wesley (29), much over three times the number of Wesley hymns used in America. This has been true because John Wesley's own society in his own land is privileged to gaze more intimately into his devout face and

> In those clear, piteous, piercing eyes behold
> The very soul that over England flamed.[1]

For generations his England has taken pride in preserving almost intact the book of the two Wesleys. Even when the omission of some of the Wesley hymns seemed necessary, the Wesleyan committee proceeded upon the principle that before a Wesley hymn be excluded they must have a good reason for its exclusion, rather than insisting upon a good reason for retaining it, thus placing the burden of proof upon the plaintiff. To the half hundred Wesley hymns thus retained, and about two hundred other hymns, also endeared to the Wesleyan Church, have been added a fine body of nearly three hundred hymns, only one of which had never been published before in any book.

These hymns have been arranged in much the same order of subjects as fixed by Wesley. The center of the book contains the body of Wesley hymns, preceded by hymns of adoration, and followed by hymns for children, sacrament, and festivals, national and philanthropic. Dr. Stephenson has commented upon

---

[1] "John Wesley," by Richard Watson Gilder.

this in his sketchy critique of the hymn book, and has pointed out that the lack of worship-hymns by Wesley is rooted in the fact that the Anglican Church had turned out the Methodists from the formal places of worship.[1]

There are many differences in the text of the same hymns, as used in England and America, due to alterations from the original made by both Churches, but more especially by the Americans. Our hymn, "Weep not for a brother deceased," they have retained in its original form, "Rejoice for a brother deceased," to which our Joint Hymnal Commission, after hours of debate, nearly changed our hymn. Some verses of the same hymn are often used by one Church, and not by the other. Our hymn, "There's a wideness in God's mercy," begins thus in the Wesleyan Hymn Book: "Was there ever kindest shepherd." Many such examples of these differences, caused by altera-tion and omission, could be cited, were it within our province.

These hymns have been set to a splendid collection of tunes, one half of them being new to the Wesleyan Church, but only a few of them never having been published before. The Conference instructed the committee to select the tunes in the first instance, and then submit them to the editor "for criticism or alterative suggestion," retaining, however, the final authority within the committee. The committee professes to have observed the canon that the tunes must be such as the people can and will sing. The

[1] See Dr. T. B. Stephenson's article in Christian Advocate, July 14, 1904.

editor expressed his ideal thus: "I would like this tune book to be the finest in the world"; and from the musical standpoint he has approached this ideal.

To our comparison of the Methodist Hymnal with other hymnals there remain to be stated briefly the superlatives; for in some points at least our American Methodist collection is unique. In the first place, on the mechanical side, the mammoth edition of 576,000 in which the Methodist Hymnal made its first appearance in 1905 was the largest first edition of any merchantable book ever issued in America.

It is the first official hymnal adopted by the Methodist Episcopal Church and the Methodist Episcopal Church, South.

Since the Methodists form the largest Protestant body in America, and the Roman Catholics do not generally use congregational singing in their worship, the Methodist Hymnal has been adopted for more millions of members than any other official hymnal in America, and probably in the world.

Of all hymnals in use it is undoubtedly the best suited to the theological beliefs of American Methodism in this age.

Musically, it surpasses all of its predecessors, and is the most adaptable to our nation-wide needs of all the high-standard hymnals now in use.

PART II
THE HYMNS

CHAPTER IV

THE STORY OF THE HYMNS

Experiences which Led to the Writing of the Hymns—
Experiences in the Use of the Hymns

Every hymn has a spiritual background in the personal experience of its author. As all literature is an expression of life, even so true hymns are the expression of an individual spiritual life, though their sentiments be adapted to universal Christian experience. It is not given to us to know the inner conflicts, the secret strivings of the soul, or the peculiar joys of each hymn-writer, that may have inspired the writing of our great hymns. Many a line, that is sung coldly or thoughtlessly, has been poured into poetic form from the molten metal of the soul's furnace. Of the real story of most of our hymns we shall never know until the final day when all secrets are revealed.

A few of the sacred poets, however, have taken us into their confidence as to the writing of their hymns, while of the lives of still others we know sufficient to determine the state of mind which produced their hymns. It is impossible within the compass of a few pages to relate more than a few of the many stories that have clustered about these seven hundred hymns. Therefore, those which are here presented have been chosen chiefly to illustrate different types of experience which have stirred men to hymnodic expression.

The conversion of a soul from sin to righteousness

has inspired the writing of many a strong evangelistic
hymn. The supreme joy of the new birth and the
ecstasy of freedom from sin have been frequently
caught up into song from the deepest emotions of the
poet's soul. Joseph Hart, the author of "Come, ye
sinners, poor and needy," had fallen away from a godly
life. His sin was made more hideous to him because
of the memory of the lost experience of Christian joy
and peace. The very tortures of his conscience kept
him from returning to the throne of grace, until, finally
contemplating the sufferings of Christ, he yielded his
life anew and for all time to the Saviour. With the
joy of a returned prodigal he wrote:

> Let not conscience make you linger,
>   Nor of fitness fondly dream;
> All the fitness he requireth
>   Is to feel your need of him,

and another verse also clearly referring to himself:

> Come, ye weary, heavy-laden,
>   Bruised and mangled by the fall;
> If you tarry till you're better,
>   You will never come at all.

Henry Kirke White, who at the age of eighteen
wrote, "When, marshaled on the nightly plain," and
died within two years afterward, might have remained a skeptic until his death but for an intimate
friend, R. W. Almond, later rector of Saint Peter's,
Nottingham. After Almond became a Christian he
shunned White as a dangerous companion, and when
White complained of his studied absence Almond told
him the reason. With horror and resentment White

replied, "Great God! you surely think worse of me than I deserve!" But into the blackness of that experience and his consequent conviction of sin there shone the Star of Bethlehem, and in this hymn the youthful poet sings of the Star as his guide through raging seas, where

> Deep horror then my vitals froze,
> Death-struck, I ceased the tide to stem,

until at last the ship of his soul was "safely moored, my perils o'er."

Charles Wesley, many of whose hymns were directly autobiographical, was at his best in singing of the work of redemption as he had felt it. Immediately after his conversion in 1738 he wrote the hymn beginning:

> And can it be that I should gain
> An interest in my Saviour's blood?

In one verse he sums up the whole wonderful story:

> Long my imprisoned spirit lay,
> Fast bound in sin and nature's night;
> Thine eye diffused a quickening ray,
> I woke, the dungeon flamed with light:
> My chains fell off, my heart was free,
> I rose, went forth, and followed thee.

This is thought to be the hymn mentioned by John Wesley in telling of his own conversion at ten o'clock in the evening, after which they went to Charles's room in Little Britain, where "we sung the hymn with great joy, and parted with prayer."

Charles Wesley had a fondness for observing anniversaries in a devout fashion. He always wrote a hymn upon his birthday. And so it is not strange that one of his greatest hymns was written upon the first anniversary of his conversion, May 21, 1739. These words, beginning "O for a thousand tongues to sing," have become so endeared to all Methodists that they have formed the first hymn in all the important Methodist hymnals in Great Britain and America. The very first phrase is said to have been suggested by the remark of Peter Böhler to Wesley in praise of Christ, "Had I a thousand tongues, I would praise Him with them all!" The line, "'Tis life and health and peace," is suggestive of Wesley's serious sickness mentioned in his own account of his conversion in the home of one Thomas Bray: "I was composing myself to sleep and quietness and peace, when I heard one come and say, 'In the name of Jesus of Nazareth, arise and believe, and thou shalt be healed of all thine infirmities!' The words struck me to the heart. I lay musing and trembling. With a strange palpitation of heart, I said, yet feared to say, 'I believe, I believe!'" When at last he won the consciousness of sins forgiven, he prayed, and then read from the Bible this passage: "He hath put a new song in my mouth," which sentiment is echoed in the line, "'Tis music in the sinner's ears." Then, as the flood of memory of this great day sweeps over him on its first anniversary, he exclaims:

> He breaks the power of canceled sin,
> He sets the prisoner free;
> His blood can make the foulest clean;
> His blood availed for me.

Count Nicolaus L. Zinzendorf, the Moravian preacher, is said to have been converted through

beholding and meditating upon the famous painting,
"Ecce Homo," in the Düsseldorf Gallery, portraying
Christ's bowed head crowned with thorns. Something
of his intense vision of Christ's sufferings is caught in
John Wesley's translation of Zinzendorf's hymn be-
ginning: "Jesus, thy blood and righteousness" (148).
Its relation to his own salvation the author sings in our
fourth verse:

> Lord, I believe thy precious blood
> For me, e'en for my soul was shed.

The fact that this hymn was written upon a voyage
from the West Indies to England early in the year
1739 makes more interesting his references to the
ocean in the last verse:

> were sinners more
> Than sands upon the ocean's shore,
> Thou hast for all a ransom paid.

The joy of seeing a whole houseful of friends converted in answer to her prayer, while on a little visit of
five days to Areley House, led Frances Ridley Havergal to write (348):

> Take my life, and let it be
> Consecrated, Lord, to thee.

Of this she said: "The last night of my visit I was
too happy to sleep, and passed most of the night in
praise and renewal of my own consecration, and these
little couplets formed themselves and chimed in my
heart, one after another, till they finished with, 'Ever,
only, all for thee.'"[1] Her method of work she once

---

[1] From "Frances Ridley Havergal," by the Rev. E. Davies, p. 61 and p. 40.

described thus: "Writing is praying with me, for I never seem to write even a verse by myself, and feel like a little child writing: you know a child would look up at every sentence and say, 'And what shall I say next?'"

Similarly, Mrs. Elizabeth Codner, hearing of many wonderful conversions through a revival in Ireland, wrote in 1860: "Lord, I hear of showers of blessing," in order that her unconverted friends, to whom she sent the verses, might utter as their own prayer, "Even me, even me!"

In contrast to the joy of the soul's conversion, now and then is heard a note of anxiety, lest the paths of sin lure the soul away from God. The Rev. Robert Robinson's "Come, thou Fount of every blessing" contains a passage which, in the light of his later life, speaks eloquently of his conflict of soul:

> Prone to wander, Lord, I feel it,
> Prone to leave the God I love.

Years after he wrote this, when he had drifted into frivolous ways, a stranger once quoted the verses to him; and full of emotion he replied: "I am the unhappy man who composed that hymn, many years ago, and I would give a thousand worlds, if I had them, to enjoy the feelings I then had."

"Lead, kindly Light, amid th' encircling gloom," is a prayer for divine guidance in the midst of the gloom of spiritual perplexity. Whether or not it was written on a ship becalmed for a foggy week in the Straits of Bonifacio, between Corsica and Sardinia, as some have told us, surely and eloquently it reveals the author's hesitant, beclouded state of mind and spirit at this period of his life. A minister of the Church of England, Dr. John H. Newman, had become anxious because of the spiritual indifference in his own Church. In his recent visit to the Continent, and more especially in Rome, from which he was now returning, he had felt more strongly than ever before the lure of Romanism, which, finally, a decade later, led him to enter the Roman Catholic Church, and still later to become cardinal in 1879. "The night is dark, and I am far from home" expresses his spiritual unrest, if not homesickness for old England. "One step enough for me" was the guiding principle of his progress during those dark years. The whole second verse is biographical in regretting that willfulness which he confesses in other verse written earlier upon this visit to the Continent:

> Time was I shrank from what was right,
>   For fear of what was wrong.

> *   *   *   *

> Such dread of sin was indolence,
>   Such aim at heaven was pride.

> *   *   *   *

> So, when my Saviour calls, I rise,
>   And calmly do my best.

But through it all there shines the faith of the great soul that "thy power," the guide of wandering souls, "will lead me on" till "the night is gone." Cardinal Newman denied the authorship of the fourth verse of

"Lead, kindly Light," sometimes attributed to him. The accompanying illustration reproduces this denial in his own handwriting, although it is uttered in the third person.

The intensity of spiritual emotion that impelled Cardinal Newman to write this wonderful hymn we can scarcely begin to understand.   Dr. Ray Palmer says of the writing of his hymn, "My faith looks up to thee": "I gave form to what I felt by writing with little effort the stanzas.   I recollect I wrote them with very tender emotion, and ended the last line with tears."   Fanny Crosby thus relates the story of writing one of her hymns: "While I sat there that evening the line came to me, 'Rescue the perishing, care for the dying.'   I could think of nothing else that night. When I arrived at my home I went to work at once, and before I retired the entire hymn was ready for a melody."

The chastening, humbling influences of illness bring the truly consecrated soul nearer to God.   Miss Katherine Hankey had passed through a severe illness of many months, and was still in helpless weakness, when she wrote, "Tell me the old, old story."   Thus from the heart she exclaims:

> For I am weak and weary,
> And helpless and defiled.

How naturally the convalescent's mind dwells upon

> That wonderful Redemption,
> God's remedy for sin.

The hymn, "Father, whate'er of earthly bliss," was written by Miss Anna Steele during an illness.   The

Jan.y 5. 1881

Cardinal Newman

begs to inform the Rev. G. Hepburn

that the fourth Stanza added to

"Lead Kindly Light" is none of

his : and added with no leave

of mikis, and that, on his remon-

-strance, the author of it has with-

-drawn it from his Edition, in which

it appeared.

poem, entitled "Desiring Resignation and Thankful-
ness," originally began thus:

> When I survey life's varied scene
> Amid the darkest hours.

It is the Christian sufferer who is singing in the lines:

> Give me a calm, a thankful heart,
> From every murmur free.

The words and music of "Tell it out among the
nations" were written by Miss Frances Ridley Havergal in Wales during a severe illness, as she was listening
to the church bells calling to service.   The theme was
suggested by a phrase she had just read in her Prayer
Book, "Tell it out among the heathen that the Lord is
King."   From her own weariness that Sabbath morning she sang, "Tell it out among the weary ones what
rest he gives."

Something of the inspiration through sympathy
with sickness and its hallowing influences may be
gleaned from Richard Baxter's quaint note to his
hymn, "Lord, it belongs not to my care;" for he added
this line: "This Covenant my dear Wife in her former
Sickness subscribed with a chearful will.   Job 12. 26."

The sense of the certainty of approaching death
arouses no terrors in the heart of the Christian, who
yearns for the homeland.   The Rev. Thomas R.
Taylor was warned of the disease that must soon
claim his life.   But, undaunted by the prospect, he
wrote that hymn of heaven:

> I'm but a stranger here,
> Heaven is my home.

One line, "Short is my pilgrimage," was all too prophetic, for he died at the age of twenty-seven. But so heroic was his fight in the Master's cause during those last months in the valley of the shadow of death that James Montgomery was thereby inspired to write our hymn, "Servant of God, well done."

Charles Wesley wrote, "Who are these arrayed in white?" as a eulogy upon his parents shortly after their death.

Under mortal shadow was written the great hymn for the dying Christian, "Abide with me," by the Rev. Henry Francis Lyte, minister to Brixham, Devonshire, England. The disease of consumption had overtaken him past the half-century milestone of his active life, and the doctors had insisted that he leave for Italy. On his last Sabbath in his old parish, September 5, 1847, against the protest of his friends, he preached and administered the sacrament of the Lord's Supper. The effort nearly exhausted him, but after resting in the afternoon he was able to walk at twilight all alone by the sea. Here on this walk the thoughts of his coming departure from England and probably from human life came thronging upon his mind, and in that hour of hallowed devotion he conceived the hymn:

> Abide with me!   Fast falls the eventide,
> The darkness deepens—Lord, with me abide!
> When other helpers fail, and comforts flee,
> Help of the helpless, O abide with me!

The verses, "Swift to its close ebbs out life's little day," and "Hold thou thy cross before my closing eyes," reveal his sense of impending death; but with what courage and faith it was blended is proven in the lines:

> Where is death's sting? where, grave, thy victory?
> I triumph still, if thou abide with me.

The next day he started for the Riviera, which he never reached, for in less than eleven weeks he died in Nice, November 20, 1847.

The last poem of Charles Wesley's was composed and uttered upon his deathbed. Being "in feebleness extreme," he called to Mrs. Wesley and asked to write down these lines, which he dictated:

> In age and feebleness extreme,
> Who shall a sinful worm redeem?
> Jesus, my only hope thou art,
> Strength of my failing flesh and heart;
> O, could I catch a smile from thee,
> And drop into eternity!

A hymn that has comforted many a soul at the threshold of heaven is "One sweetly solemn thought," about which Miss Phœbe Cary, who wrote it, once said: "I composed it in the little back third-story bedroom, one Sunday morning, after coming from Church." The hallowed thoughts of the sanctuary were woven into the noble poem.

Thus we have considered a few of the hymns that have voiced intense spiritual experiences, largely induced by subjective causes. Frequently, however, some external cause, some critical event, some calamity has revealed to the poet an undreamed vision of divine truth; and with a new sense of his relation to

God he has poured forth his heart in the living lines of an exalted hymn.

The calamity of blindness in banishing physical light from the afflicted has often opened to the soul new flood-gates of spiritual light. "Come, O my soul! in sacred lays" was written by a blind man, the Rev. Thomas Blacklock. It is not strange that his conception of heaven was of a place of ineffable, eternal light, as we see in the second verse (23):

> Enthroned amid the radiant spheres,
> He glory like a garment wears;
> To form a robe of light divine,
> Ten thousand suns around him shine.

In the hymns of Fanny Crosby, the aged blind singer, is expressed this same pathetic yearning for light. In one hymn she prays: "Lead me through the vale of shadows" (332); in another (490):

> Till my soul is lost in love
> In a brighter, brighter world above.

In "Blessed Assurance" (548) she sings of

>   . . .   perfect delight!
> Visions of rapture burst on my sight.

Likewise the blind English clergyman, William W. Walford, sang of the vision of his heavenly home (516):

>   . . .   Sweet hour of prayer,
> May I thy consolation share,
> Till from Mount Pisgah's lofty height,
> *I view my home.*   . . .

The story is told, though not without question, that the great scholar and preacher, George Matheson, was at one time betrothed to marry a young woman, when the physicians one day told him that his long-fought disease of the eyes must soon result in total blindness. In a spirit of love and frankness he told her of his impending sorrow, of his great love for her, but of his willingness to release her from her promise, if she so desired. Her decision to break the engagement only intensified his sorrow, and might have driven him to despair, had he not cast himself upon the love of Christ, and found the divine relief which he so pathetically expresses in his hymn:

> O Love that wilt not let me go,
>   I rest my weary soul in thee;
> I give thee back the life I owe,
> That in thine ocean depths its flow
>   May richer, fuller be.
>
> O Light that followest all my way,
>   I yield my flickering torch to thee;
> My heart restores its borrowed ray,
> That in thy sunshine's blaze its day
>   May brighter, fairer be.

Of the writing of this hymn Matheson said: "I was sitting alone in my study in a state of great mental depression caused by a real calamity. My hymn was the voice of my depression. It was not made for utilitarian purposes; it was wrung out spontaneously from the heart. All the other verses I have written are manufactured articles; this came like a dayspring from on high."

A grief similar to George Matheson's was suffered by Joseph Scriven, whose betrothed was drowned shortly before the day fixed for their wedding. The intense sorrow, into which his joy was so suddenly changed,

only drove him closer to the Divine Friend; for he
wrote:

> What a friend we have in Jesus,
> All our sins and griefs to bear!

So universally true and helpful is the sentiment of
this hymn that it has been printed nearly ten million
times.

The hardship of imprisonment in the Convent of
Saint Marie, Paris, 1686, in Vincennes, 1695, and in
the Bastille, 1698–1702, was imposed upon Madame
Jeanne Marie Bouviers de la Mothe Guyon, because of
her religious beliefs.   Nor was this hardship any less,
since her child had died, her own beauty had been
blighted by smallpox, her mother-in-law had turned
against her, and severest criticism had been passed
upon her creeds by many theological leaders.   In
what spirit this leader of the Quietist movement and
friend of Fenelon bore her tribulations we may know
from her lines:

> My Lord, how full of sweet content
> I pass my years of banishment!

Helen Maria Williams was a resident in Paris when
the Bastille fell in 1789, and she was imprisoned in the
Temple as a foreign suspect until the death of Robes-
pierre.   Her reliance upon divine help during these
days of anxiety is expressed in her hymn, "While
thee I seek, protecting Power."   It was immediately
after all of Isaac Watts's property had been destroyed
by fire that he wrote, "Come, sound his praise abroad."
In the line, "We are his works and not our own," he
acknowledges that all that we are and have belongs to

God. Such Christian philosophy makes our material losses seem trivial.

To a sensitive soul the misunderstanding of noble motives brings a keenness of pain, rarely suspected by the accusers. Every evening at twilight Mrs. Phœbe Hinsdale Brown stole away from her four children to a grove near by for prayer and meditation, because in their poverty they were living in an unfinished house in Ellington, Connecticut, with a sick sister in the only finished room. To the gossipers, who for this daily absence persecuted her with false accusations, she replied in the lines,

> I love to steal awhile away
> From little ones and care,

which, modified, and shortened, has become our hymn (498).

The virulent opposition that the Wesleys met in preaching anew the doctrines of regeneration by faith is hard to understand in this day of free speech. Churchmen called them ranting enthusiasts or secret Papists. Hardened sinners reviled them. Sometimes they were stoned by the mob, sometimes arrested by the authorities. On one occasion a man kept interrupting Charles Wesley's sermon with vile epithets and mockery. At last Wesley silenced him with a scathing denunciation of the man's sin. The sermon proceeded, and the divine message won the hearts of many in the audience. Upon retiring from the meeting Wesley wrote, "Jesus, the name high over all" (222).

Very different were the emotions of the Rev. Dr.

John Fawcett when he produced his most famous hymn, "Blest be the tie that binds." Having received, in 1772, a call to leave his charge in the Baptist church of Wainsgate to become pastor of a large London church, he was about to go when his people, broken-hearted, besought him and finally persuaded him to remain, though his personal property was all ready for shipment. He said to them, "You may unpack my goods, and we will live lovingly together for the Lord." Thus came to be written the great hymn of Christian unity; for he had learned that "When we asunder part, it gives us inward pain," and henceforth both pastor and people decided to "Share our mutual woes, Our mutual burdens bear," throughout the rest of life.

Just as orators have arisen in the might of their eloquence to command the thought of some great occasion, even so our sacred poets in their purpose to stir the emotions and direct the thought of some great religious gathering, have sometimes produced hymns that have outlived the occasions for which they were written—occasions that are now remembered only because of their hymns.

Such a hymn is the Christmas song, "Hail to the Lord's anointed," written by James Montgomery for a gathering of the British Moravians on Christmas Day, 1821. "Jesus, where'er thy people meet," was written by Cowper upon the occasion of the removal of the prayer meeting at Olney to another building. "Lord, while for all mankind we pray," was composed in 1837 as an English national anthem by the Rev.

John R. Wreford at the time of Queen Victoria's coronation.   Dr. John James Bonar, of Saint Andrew's Free Church, Greenock, was accustomed to print a little memorandum for each communion service in his church.   For one of these he asked his brother, Dr. Horatius Bonar, to write a hymn; and for this coming Sabbath was written, in two days, the hymn for the Lord's Supper, "Here, O my Lord, I see thee face to face."   "Thou, whose unmeasured temple stands," by William Cullen Bryant, owes its existence to the dedication of a chapel on Prince Street, New York, in 1835.   In its original form it began, "O Thou, whose own vast temple stands."   The most popular American poet of his times was asked to write a hymn of dedication for the Hanover Street Church, Boston, and the result was the lines beginning, "The perfect world by Adam trod," by Nathaniel P. Willis.   "Saviour, again to thy dear name we raise," by the Rev. John Ellerton, was produced in 1866 for the Parochial Choirs Festival at Nantwich, Cheshire; and "Forward, be our watchword," was written in June, 1871, by Dean Henry Alford for the Tenth Festival of Parochial Choirs of the Canterbury Diocesan Union.

Dean Shipley, of Saint Asaph, was about to preach a missionary sermon on Whitsunday, 1819, for the Society for the Propagation of the Gospel in Foreign Parts.   The day before, he asked his son-in-law, Reginald Heber, rector of Hodnet, to write "something for them to sing in the morning."   In a very short time he completed the great hymn "From Greenland's icy mountains," which was sung the next morning.

Dr. Samuel Wolcott's "Christ for the world we sing" also owes its birth to a missionary occasion, though in this instance it was written after the meeting, February 7, 1869, from which the writer was returning alone through the streets when these lines came to him.   In his own words the story is told: "The Young Men's Christian Association of Ohio met in one of our churches with their motto in evergreen letters over the pulpit, 'Christ for the World and the World for Christ.'   This suggested the hymn, 'Christ for the world we sing.' "

Similarly, it was immediately after a conference-room talk on the twenty-third psalm, and while still in the spirit of the occasion, that the Rev. Joseph H. Gilmore, in 1861, wrote, "He leadeth me," in the home of a friend in Philadelphia, where he was visiting while supplying a Baptist pulpit in that city.

A legend, containing only the three words "Sleeping in Jesus," inscribed on a tombstone in the cemetery of Pennycross Chapel in Devonshire, led Margaret Mackay to write for The Amethyst of Edinburgh the beautiful funeral hymn, "Asleep in Jesus."

The poetic inspirations derived from nature, stirring the human soul and suggesting divine truth, have not left hymnology wholly uninfluenced.   The stars, the sea, the earth with its mountains, hills, plains, and rivers, its flowers and birds, winter storms and harvests of "full corn," with the "bright blue sky" above it—all these are portrayed within our Hymnal, and evidence the poets' visions of beauty in nature.   We are told that Isaac Watts wrote his hymn of heaven,

"There is a land of pure delight," while in Southampton, England, and that his view of the Isle of Wight across the River Itchen suggested the familiar lines:

> Sweet fields beyond the swelling flood
>   Stand dressed in living green;
> So to the Jews old Canaan stood,
>   While Jordan rolled between.

The South of England is pictured in another hymn, "Lo! on a narrow neck of land," which Charles Wesley is said to have written at Land's End in Cornwall. Some have maintained that this hymn was written upon a foreign journey, but even so, it must have been reminiscent of Land's End, which Wesley had frequently visited.

We have already referred to the tradition which attributes much of the imagery of "Lead, kindly Light," to the scenes upon a voyage on the Mediterranean. More trustworthy is the narrative concerning Joseph Addison's hymn. Returning from the terrors of a voyage on the Mediterranean Sea, he gives us from his own recent experiences a picture of the Christian traveler's gratitude in his hymn, "How are thy servants blest, O Lord!" which is embodied in his essay on "The Sea," in the Spectator, No. 489, in 1712. The second verse describes the hardships through which he had safely passed:

> In foreign realms, and lands remote,
>   Supported by thy care,
> Through burning climes they pass unhurt,
>   And breathe in tainted air.

Again in a description of the retiring storm he says:

> The storm is laid, the winds retire,
>   Obedient to thy will;
> The sea, that roars at thy command,
>   At thy command is still.

It was the same vivid memory of travels in Palestine a few months before that enabled Bishop Phillips Brooks to touch our imaginations in his exquisite Christmas hymn, so that we almost behold the very birthplace of Christ, as we sing:

> O little town of Bethlehem, how still we see thee lie!
> Above thy deep and dreamless sleep the silent stars go by;
> Yet in thy dark streets shineth the everlasting Light;
> The hopes and fears of all the years are met in thee to-
>   night.

Dean Arthur P. Stanley's

> O Master, it is good to be
> High on the mountain here with thee,

was written after his visit in 1853 to Palestine. Of Bishop Ken's "Evening Hymn" Theron Brown says, "The 'Evening Hymn' drew scenic inspiration, it is told, from the lovely view in Horningsham Park at 'Heaven's Gate Hill,' "[1] while the author was walking to and from church in the twilight. Still another night scene, portrayed in hymn lines, was the night glow in the sky from the great fires of the Newcastle Collieries, which Charles Wesley was visiting, in order to preach to the colliers. Likening this to the gospel fires, he sang:

> See how great a flame aspires,
>   Kindled by a spark of grace!

---

[1] "The Story of the Hymns and Tunes," by Theron Brown and Hezekiah Butterworth.

Jesus' love the nations fires,
   Sets the kingdoms on a blaze:
To bring fire on earth he came;
   Kindled in some hearts it is:
O that all might catch the flame,
   All partake the glorious bliss!

The stone quarry in the Isle of Portland was a great industry, peculiar to the town where he was preaching at the time, that suggested a hymn to Charles Wesley. Before preaching to the quarrymen he wrote:

Come, O thou all victorious Lord,
   Thy power to us make known;
Strike with the *hammer* of thy word,
   And break these *hearts of stone,*

a figure of speech that must have stirred the imaginations of the workmen.

Not all the interesting stories of our hymns center about their origin; for with the use of the hymns thousands of thrilling memories are associated, recalling scenes when the quoting or singing of a hymn has stirred the deepest emotions of the soul.

Could the hymns in our Methodist Hymnal recite the story of all the deathbeds they have cheered, what a wonderful testimony to the faith and fearlessness of the dying Christian would be told! Isaac Watts wrote (in hymn No. 581):

Jesus can make a dying-bed
   Feel soft as downy pillows are,
While on his breast I lean my head,
   And breathe my life out sweetly there.

In many a Christian home where this miracle has

been wrought, there are cherished among the tenderest memories

> Those sweet, fervent hymns
> Made sacred by how many saints of God,
> Who breathed their souls out on the well-loved tones.[1]

The story is sometimes repeated in the writer's home of the last words of Great-grandfather Miller, whose saintly life was crowned with a triumphant death. Surrounded by his sorrowing family, his dying request was that they sing his favorite hymn, "There is a fountain filled with blood." But so great was their grief they could scarcely sing, and when they reached the end of the fourth verse, "And shall until I die," their voices broke down. Then, gathering up what little strength he had left, he sang the last verse alone:

> "Then in a nobler, sweeter song,
> I'll sing thy power to save,
> When this poor lisping, stammering tongue
> Lies silent in the grave."

And with these words his body fell back, while his soul took up the nobler, sweeter song.

One of the earliest accounts of a hymn being sung by a departing Christian relates to the death of the Venerable Bede, on May 26, in the year 735. He requested his sorrowing friends to carry him to that part of the room where he had always prayed; and there he sang the Gloria Patri, beginning with feeble voice, "Glory be to the Father," and continuing until with his last breath he uttered, "world without end."

Many Methodist saints, who have been canonized

---

[1] By Richard Watson Gilder.

at least in the affections of the Church, have expressed by some hymn the joy of passing to the larger life. John Wesley, the day before he died, sang the first two verses of Watts's old hymn:

> I'll praise my Maker while I've breath,
> And when my voice is lost in death,
>   Praise shall employ my nobler powers.

Bishop Hedding, who died in New York, April 29, 1852, spoke in his last words of the ineffable joy of fifty years of service for the Master. "I want to tell it to all the world!" he exclaimed. "O, that I had a trumpet voice!

> 'Then would I tell to sinners round
> What a dear Saviour I have found.' "

Dr. Nathan Bangs in his last illness quoted the third verse of our hymn (371):

> The promised land, from Pisgah's top,
>   I now exult to see:
> My hope is full, O glorious hope!
>   Of immortality.

Bishop Matthew Simpson, shortly before his death, in 1884, quoted this verse:

> O, would he more of heaven bestow!
>   And when the vessels break
> Let our triumphant spirits go
>   To grasp the God we seek;
> In rapturous awe on him to gaze,
>   Who bought the sight for me;
> And shout and wonder at his grace,
>   To all eternity.

The last line he repeated over and over again. His last audible words were, "Yes! yes! glory be to Jesus!"

A most pathetic but appropriate use of an old, familiar hymn is the story of the deathbed of the Rev. Thomas Stockton. He had fallen into a sleep, which his sorrowing friends thought was his last. But just before he died, he awakened, looked upon them and said:

> "And are we yet alive,
>   And see each other's face?"

Many a statesman or leader in public life, humbled to pass through the same way we all must tread, has departed this life with hymns of faith upon his lips. Thus Cobden died, repeating John Wesley's hymn:

> "What though my flesh and heart decay?
> Thee shall I love in endless day!"

Prince Albert, Queen Victoria's royal consort, in his last moments quoted "Rock of Ages," and President McKinley uttered lines from "Nearer, my God, to thee," as he was dying; and each of these hymns echoed throughout the two brother Anglo-Saxon nations. Wordsworth's daughter was comforted at the approach of death by the hymn, "Just as I am," which had been repeated to her every morning for two months previous. Jerome of Prague, marching to his execution, sang: "Welcome, happy morning."

Sometimes a poet on his deathbed has been comforted by the lines of a hymn written by himself. The Rev. Sir Henry Williams Baker, as he was dying on February 12, 1877, spoke in clear, hopeful tones a part of his own hymn on the twenty-third psalm,

"The King of love my Shepherd is," which bears these lines:

> In death's dark vale I fear no ill
> With thee, dear Lord, beside me.

His last words were,

> "And on his shoulder gently laid,
> And home, rejoicing, brought me."

Likewise, Frances Ridley Havergal at the very close of a life of tender, courageous witnessing for the Master, sang a verse of her hymn, which begins, "Golden harps are sounding"; and after a convulsive sickness she whispered, "There, now, it's all over," as the "Pearly gates were opened" for her soul.

Dr. George J. Stevenson's volume, "The Methodist Hymn Book and Its Associations," is a treasury of the triumphant dying words of godly men and women who were Wesleyan Methodists in England. Among these are some fourscore hymns in our own collection, from which lines of triumph and faith have been uttered in the dying moments of the devout. How clearly and tenderly our hymns, even those not classed as hymns of heaven, express the thought and sentiment of that solemnly joyful hour of death may be seen from such phrases as these, each well accepted as the last words spoken or sung by some Christian. They are here arranged in logical order:

> Teach me to die, that so I may
> Rise glorious on the judgment day (49).

> Then pain
> Is sweet, and life or death is gain (335).

> But there's a nobler rest above (73).

> In death as life be thou my guide,
> And save me, who for me hast died (333).

> Happy, if with my latest breath
> I may but gasp his name (222).

> Into thy arms I fall (268).

> The clouds disperse, the shadows fly;
> The Invisible appears in sight,
> And God is seen by mortal eye (298).

> The opening heavens around me shine
> With beams of sacred bliss (535).

> And angels beckon me away,
> And Jesus bids me come (624).

> Our shelter from the stormy blast,
> And our eternal home (577).

> There all the ship's company meet,
> Who sailed with the Saviour beneath (594).

> There we shall see his face,
> And never, never sin (22).

> Through all eternity to thee
> A grateful song I'll raise (105).

These, and many, many other similar passages, have cheered a host of departing pilgrims, and will long be remembered as

> The hymns with which they passed away from earth
> In long-gone centuries, that backward sweep.[1]

The great variety of conditions under which hymns have been used as prayers is remarkable. The writer never so fully realized the power of a hymn, uttered in prayer, as upon one summer morning

---

[1] From " Alma Vista," by Lebbeus Harding Rogers.

near Intervale in the White Mountains. We paused
at a farmhouse to inquire the way up the mountain.
An old, old man opened the door, his head crowned
with thick, snow-white hair, his face a benediction of
goodness. When he had told us the way we inquired
if he knew the great Guide to the heavenly road. His
answer was the story of his life in brief, a life devoted
to the Master's service in preaching, teaching, and
living the gospel. Before we continued our tramp he
asked us to kneel with him to pray, and with an infinite earnestness, and in every phrase a strange pathos
and power, he poured out his heart in the lines:

> When I survey the wondrous cross
> On which the Prince of glory died.

All four verses he recited, and this alone was his prayer,
one of the most eloquent petitions we had ever heard.

An ancient Methodist illustration of the effective
use of hymns in soul-winning was the conversion of
Sarah Baker, of Tiverton in England, while after his
sermon, Mr. Rouse, a local preacher, was reading the
line, "This is the time, no more delay." Instances of
conversions, such as this, are the most practical argu-
ments in favor of the time-honored custom of reading
hymns before singing, in order to more deeply impress
the thought of the words. Similarly, the Rev. Samuel
Wesley's hymn, "Behold the Saviour of mankind,"
while being read at a love feast, led Owen Davis, a
Welshman, to accept the atonement of Christ, and,
yielding his life to the Master's service, he became one
of John Wesley's effective preachers. The original
manuscript of this hymn, no copy being then in exist-

ence, was almost miraculously saved by being blown out of the window during the fire that burned the Epworth Rectory to the ground, August 24, 1709.

Sometimes by reading a hymn in private, a soul has been awakened to conviction and repentance. Thus a Walkeringham teacher, William Morris, was converted by reading the lines beginning: "Stung by the scorpion sin," in the hymn, "Let heaven and earth agree." In the quietude of family devotions, John Watson, of Yorkshire, joined in the singing of "Welcome, sweet day of rest." The lines,

> One day amidst the place
> Where my dear Lord has been
> Is better than ten thousand days
> Of pleasurable sin,

became engraved upon his conscience, and, retiring to solitude, he gave his heart and life to God.

Dr. Stevenson at one time compiled a record of two hundred souls who had been converted at various times during the singing of "Arise, my soul, arise." He also tells the story of a young man, a leader in social gayety, who had been persuaded by a friend to attend a Bible reading. Retiring to a saloon for revelry to stifle his conscience, he was haunted by the lines sung at the meeting:

> Come, Holy Spirit, heavenly Dove,
> With all thy quickening powers;
> Come, shed abroad a Saviour's love,
> And that shall quicken ours.

He soon left the house, and sought the pardon of God.

The wife of the Rev. John Shipman, a Wesleyan minister, attributed her conversion to the influence of the hymn, "Come, let us anew our journey pursue," as sung at a Watch-night meeting in Aberdeen, Scotland, when she was a girl.

It was through the singing of Isaac Watts's hymn, "Alas! and did my Saviour bleed," that the evangelist E. P. Hammond was converted at the age of seventeen in Southington, Connecticut.   Dr. Duffield[1] tells us of a sailor fearing the approach of death, and having no Bible to comfort him, remembered at last the hymn line: "For he was slain for us."   Then, recalling the rest of the hymn, "Come, let us join our cheerful songs," he found divine acceptance.   Other instances he gives us.   During a frightful storm the Rev. Andrew Kinsman was dining with a young man, whom he had met in company with the great Rev. George Whitefield.   Quoting to him the lines·

> "The God that reigns on high,
> And thunders when he please,"

Kinsman added,

> "This awful God is ours,
> Our Father and our Love";

and this led to the young man's conversion.

Dr. Spencer, in "Pastor's Sketches," relates a young woman's conversion to the singing of the hymn: "How sad our state by nature is!" early in one of his Sabbath services.   Her mind seized upon the lines,

> A guilty, weak, and helpless worm,
> On thy kind arms I fall,

until finally she believed and trusted the **Saviour.**

[1] "English Hymns," by Dr. George Duffield.

Fanny Crosby (Van Alstyne), the blind poet, five of whose hymns are in our Hymnal, in telling the story of her conversion, says that during a revival in the old Thirtieth Street Church, New York, in 1850, several times she had sought the Saviour at the altar; but not until one evening, November 20, did the light come. "After a prayer was offered they began to sing the grand old consecration hymn, 'Alas! and did my Saviour bleed,' and when they reached the third line of the fourth stanza, 'Here, Lord, I give myself away,' my very soul flooded with celestial light." Again, as in her hymns, the blind singer uses here the figure of light to represent salvation and eternal life.

The good ship Rothsay Castle was wrecked between Liverpool and Beaumaris in 1831, and nearly a hundred people were drowned. James Martin, a class leader from Liverpool, was clinging to a plank, from which several had dropped into the sea, when suddenly those near by heard, in his voice:

"The God that rules on high,
    That all the earth surveys,
That rides upon the stormy sky,
    And calms the roaring seas.

"This awful God is ours,
    Our Father and our Love,
He will send down his heavenly powers
    To carry us above."

After thus fearlessly facing death, he was rescued with a score of others.

Professor Dempter, of the Garrett Biblical Institute, and a company of missionaries on their way to South America were chased for three days by a pirate ship.

As the pirates approached, the ship's company went on deck, and all of them sang to the tune of "Old Hundred":

> "Before Jehovah's awful throne,
>   Ye nations bow with sacred joy;
> Know that the Lord is God alone,
>   He can create and he destroy."

While they were kneeling in prayer the enemy lay by, near the side of their vessel, then turned about, and sailed away.

John Wesley, about to preach in the market place at Chesterfield, was haled before a magistrate. But before going he said to his congregation, "Friends, sing a hymn while I am gone; I shall soon be back." And then he gave out the hymn:

> Why should the children of a King
>   Go mourning all their days?

In a short time, while they were still singing over the hymn, he returned triumphant.

A remarkable story is told by Dr. Duffield of the hymn, "All hail the power of Jesus' name." The Rev. E. P. Scott, while a missionary in India, started out, contrary to the pleas of his friends, to visit a distant tribe of murderous mountaineers. Upon first seeing him the natives pointed their spears at his heart. Expecting instant death, he brought forth his violin, and played while he sang with closed eyes, "All hail the power of Jesus' name." When he came to the verse, "Let every kindred, every tribe," he opened his eyes to find their attitude wholly changed. This was the beginning of two years and a half of blessed service in preaching Christ and teaching this tribe to "crown him Lord of all."

One of the most dramatic settings for the singing of a hymn was the occasion upon which King George of Tonga formally proclaimed his nation to be henceforth Christian, granting to them a Christian constitution. Five thousand natives on Whitsunday, 1862, assembled about their king, sang the hymn (631):

> Jesus shall reign where'er the sun
> Does his successive journeys run;
> His kingdom spread from shore to shore,
> Till moons shall wax and wane no more.

A curious use of hymns is cited by Fanny Crosby in her autobiography, "Memories of Eighty Years": "When a member of the Soldiers' Christian Union meets a comrade he says, 'Four hundred and ninety-four,' which is the number of 'God be with you till we meet again' in 'Sacred Songs and Solos'; the latter replies, 'Six farther on,' that is 500, which is the number of 'Blessed assurance.'"

The famous temperance advocate, John B. Gough, tells of his sad parting from his mother at home to sail for America. The ship, becalmed off Sandsgate, his home, was visited by many of his friends and relatives, and at last by his mother, who had been away during most of the day. When night shut down upon them and the boats were drawing away in the darkness to the shore, all joined in singing:

> Blest be the dear, uniting love,
>   Which will not let us part;
> Our bodies may far hence remove,
>   We still are one in heart.

The Rev. Dr. Samuel West, an old-time New England pastor, once won over his recalcitrant choir, which had refused to sing in the service, by giving out the hymn, "Come, ye that love the Lord," and asking all to begin with the second verse:

> Let those refuse to sing,
> Who never knew our God.

The spirit of warfare, so alien to the Christian faith, has been sometimes justified and sanctified when applied to a righteous cause; and with its heroisms are often associated the singing of hymns. "Terrible as is war," said Heine, "it yet displays the spiritual grandeur of man, daring to defy his mightiest and hereditary enemy, Death." While the ungodly man, with a grim outward stoicism, sets his face stolidly toward battle, the true Christian, fighting for some sacred cause in the name of the Prince of Peace, advances enthusiastically with a hymn in his heart and ofttimes upon his lips, and scorns death merely as the "narrow stream" that "divides that happy land from ours." In this spirit many times has a German army charged into battle, singing Luther's "Ein' feste Burg" (written in 1529), the better to "fight the good fight with all their might," the good fight of militant Protestantism. This hymn, styled by Heine "The Marseillaise of the Reformation," is known to have been sung by the army of Gustavus Adolphus before the Battle of Leipzig, in 1631, and also before the Battle of Lützen, in 1632. The Huguenots of France frequently used it during the troublous years, 1560 to 1572; and many instances are recorded of its use by regiments of Germans in the Franco-Prussian war.

"Fear not, O little flock, the foe," was composed and used as the battle song of the Swedish king, Gustavus Adolphus, in his campaign against Wallenstein for the preservation of Protestantism in Germany. Of several theories as to its authorship, the most probable one, and that accepted by the editors of our Hymnal, is that Dr. Jacob Fabricus (or Fabricius), the court chaplain, in these poetical lines paraphrased the thought and sentiment of the king, thus giving to the army a hymn, by which they conquered in the Battle of Lützen, though at the frightful cost of losing their gallant and devout commander.

Another German hymn of war times is "Now thank we all our God." Some evidence makes questionable the story that it was written as a national Te Deum after the Thirty Years' War (1618–1648). Even though it may have been written during the war, it was undoubtedly used after the Peace of Westphal as a song of deliverance by the German people, who, like its author, had suffered frightful hardships to win the war.

Oliver Cromwell's army was ridiculed as a psalm-singing rabble, though his detractors knew well that the very singing of their hymns helped to make them the one invincible army in all Europe.

In a later chapter we mention the tune "Caledonia," to which the Scottish warriors frequently sang the melody, later set to "Scots, wha hae wi' Wallace bled," as they charged upon the English foe in the effort to regain the throne for James III.

In our own land how often has the anthem, "My country, 'tis of thee," inspired a regiment of soldiers! During the Revolutionary War, long before this hymn was written, an incident occurred concerning its tune, which Dr. Duffield has repeated. A company of British soldiers entered a Long Island church and commanded the colonists to sing, "God save the king." The melody was sung, but in devotion to their consciences and to their God, the people sang the words frequently used in the earlier days to this tune, thereby confounding their enemies:

> Come, thou almighty King,
> Help us *thy* name to sing,

The Rev. Dr. James H. Perry, pastor of the Pacific Street Methodist Episcopal Church in Brooklyn, was attending Conference in the spring of 1861, when the news of the bombardment of Fort Sumter was received. He arose amid the intense excitement, and said: "I was educated by the government; it now needs my services. I shall resign my ministry and again take up my sword." He became colonel of the 48th Regiment N. Y. S. Volunteers, which was known as "Perry's Saints." The Rev. Dr. A. J. Palmer, formerly missionary secretary, tells in his book and in his famous lecture the story of his Company D in this regiment, which always went into battle singing, "I'm going home to die no more." Their comrades, therefore, nicknamed the company "The Die-no-mores."[1]

There was another hymn, "Say, brothers, will you meet us," brought from Methodist camp meetings to the army by the Second Battalion of Massachusetts Infantry, whose tune, fortunately not in our present Hymnal, exerted a wide influence in the Civil War; for to this tune the words, "John Brown's body," were sung throughout the army, and later also the "Battle Hymn of the Republic," by Julia Ward Howe.

[1] Cf. "48th Regiment State Volunteers," by A. J. Palmer. Published, 1885, by Veteran Association of the Regiment.

CHAPTER V

THE HYMN-WRITERS

ENGLISH HYMNODY—AMERICAN HYMNODY—THE
TRANSLATIONS—THE TITLES

IF the bibliography of hymnody, the body of the
hymns, and hymnology, the science of hymns, were
developed exhaustively, the study would attain to
tremendous proportions. Dr. Julian in his "Dictionary of Hymnology" says: "The total number of
Christian hymns in the two hundred or more dialects
in which they have been written or translated is not
less than four hundred thousand. When classified
into languages the greatest number are found to be
in German, English, Latin, and Greek in the order
named." Only a few hymns have survived to be
adopted by the modern Church, and a large proportion of the best of these are to be found within the
Methodist Hymnal.

To adequately tell the story of even our own
seven hundred and forty-eight hymns, with critical
accounts of their authors, the conditions under
which they were written, the publications first containing them and the dates thereof, their successive
alterations and the stories of their use—all these
legitimate inquiries of hymnology would easily ex-
pand into the proportions of a small library.
One hymnologist in Brooklyn, New York, has
attempted this with a body of hymns in common

use, and already his large manuscript volumes number forty. Having already examined a few typical hymns and their stories, we must be content with but a glimpse of some of the more prominent hymn authors, an outline of the successive periods in English hymn-writing, together with a statement of our debt to the hymns of foreign languages.

The foundations of English hymnody rest largely upon the metrical versions of the Psalms, which, together with other scriptural translations, were long regarded as the only hymn-forms permissible in divine worship. These we shall discuss later, along with other translations from the Hebrew. Though there were many original English hymns before his time, the first great hymnist of England represented in our Hymnal was Bishop Thomas Ken (1637–1711), who wrote the "Morning Hymn" (44), "Evening Hymn" (49), and the Doxology (718), "Praise God, from whom all blessings flow," all of which appeared first in his "Manual of Prayers for the Winchester Scholars," 1700. The good bishop, arrested with six other bishops by James II, and later under William of Orange harassed by political intrigue, would not compromise his principles to gain political preferment, and hence was forced into retirement. Of him Macaulay said in his "History of England": "He was a man of parts and learning, of quick sensibility and stainless virtue. His elaborate works have long been forgotten, but his morning and evening hymns are still

repeated daily in thousands of dwellings." In his
retirement Bishop Ken wrote these lines:

> I gladly wars ecclesiastic fly,
> Whene'er contentious spirits I descry:
> Eased of my sacred load, I live content,
> In hymns, not in disputes, my passions vent.

Three great authors of his century are represented
in the Hymnal by three great hymns, "Teach me, my
God and King" (417), by George Herbert (1593–1632);
"The Lord will come and not be slow" (642), a translation by John Milton (1608–74); and "Lord, it belongs not to my care" (470), by Richard Baxter (1615–
91), the celebrated author of "Saints' Rest."

In the model style of the brilliant Joseph Addison
(1672–1719) we have three hymns, each of them
from his famous periodical, "The Spectator":
"The spacious firmament on high" (84), being
from "Spectator" No. 465, 1712; "How are thy
servants blest, O Lord" (102), from No. 489, 1712;
and "When all thy mercies, O my God" (105), from
No. 453, 1712.

The Preface to the Methodist Hymnal announces
that it contains, besides the Wesley hymns, "the
choicest work of the other hymn-writers of the eighteenth century, Doddridge, Watts, Cowper, Newton,
Montgomery." The first of these, in chronology, in
some points of excellence, and in the number of
hymns in our collection (fifty-three, next to Charles
Wesley's the highest number), was the Rev. Dr. Isaac
Watts (1674–1748). Born in a nonconformist family,
in severest times of religious persecution, he dis-

plays a militant dogmatism on the side of Calvinism in much of his work. But, nevertheless, his devout and earnest thought, cast in the mold of scriptural phrase, and making use of the simplest English words, has won for him the title, "The Father of English Hymns." The Watts translations from the Psalms are mentioned on a later page. His hymn, "When I survey the wondrous cross" (141), was styled by Matthew Arnold "the greatest hymn in the English language." Next in the number of our hymns (twenty-two) stands the Rev. Dr. Philip Doddridge (1702–51), theologian and poet, who is best known to Methodists by his hymn, "O happy day, that fixed my choice." Even more than Watts he confined his poems to scriptural phrase. For twenty years he was pastor in a Northampton nonconformist church, at the same time writing voluminously and teaching young theologians vigorously.

The Rev. John Newton (1725–1807) and William Cowper (1731–1800), though younger than the Wesleys, lived and worked as their contemporaries. From the former we have thirteen hymns, from the latter ten. Newton was converted from a violent life of sin while at sea, and, returning to England, he gave his life to an active ministry, keeping in touch with the Wesleys and their work. In his residence at Olney as curate, he became associated with Cowper in writing "The Olney Hymns." Cowper's life had been redeemed from a life of despair to

> A season of clear shining,
> To cheer it after rain,

(to use his own phrase in hymn 454); and, though later his temperamental morbidness would sometimes unbalance his mind, he sang through his sorrow the same redemption and with the same intensity as Newton. Cowper's "There is a fountain filled with blood" (291), and Newton's "Glorious things of thee are spoken" (210), have long been great favorites in Methodist worship.

The last of these five names, James Montgomery (1771–1854), belongs more to the nineteenth than to the eighteenth century. Nineteen of his four hundred hymns are in our collection. A Scotchman so radical in his politics as to be twice cast into prison, an editor and literary critic, he will long be remembered for his Christian piety and its beautiful expression in such hymns as "Behold! the Christian warrior stands" (397) "In the hour of trial" (431), or "Prayer is the soul's sincere desire" (497).

The greatest of all English hymn-writers was Charles Wesley, greatest in the prodigious number of hymns that he wrote (said to be over sixty-five hundred within fifty years), greatest in his statement of doctrine and the earnestness of his zeal, and greatest in his high poetic expression of an intense love for the Saviour. His hymns in the Methodist Hymnal are one hundred and twenty-nine, or about one sixth of the book. The eighteenth child in the Wesley family, he came near to being adopted by a wealthy Irish gentleman. But he did not leave his family, until he made the journey to Georgia with his brother, John. After his conversion and a brief stay in Islington as curate, he joined his brother's great work for the rest of his life. Their relaton to the Church of England caused a difference of opinion on the subject between the two brothers; but as preachers and as hymn-writers both remained loyal and tremendously active in advancing the cause of Methodism.

The Wesleys were the most remarkable family in the annals of hymnology. The father of John and Charles, the Rev. Samuel Wesley (1662–1735), an intensely earnest clergyman of the Church of England, passed through a series of hardships both in providing for his large family from a meager income and in facing the bitter opposition of his fellow townsmen at Epworth, that would have overwhelmed a less courageous man. His writings in prose were voluminous; and of his poetry we still preserve in our Hymnal his lines: "Behold the Saviour of mankind" (142). His wife, Susanna Wesley, through the remarkable influence of her piety upon her children, has won the title, "The Mother of Methodism." Four of their children became poets of a high order. From the Rev. Samuel Wesley, the younger, and his sister, Mehetabel Wesley, we possess no hymns in our Hymnal, though many hymns from the former are now in use in England, while from the sacred poetry of the latter many verses could well be used as hymns.

While Charles was the greatest hymn-writer, John Wesley (1703–91) was in other respects the greater man; for through his marvelous genius for organization, his infinite capacity for work, and his ability as a preacher he exerted the greatest influence of any man upon his generation in England. And withal he excelled as a hymn-writer. Over thirty translations he made from the German, French, and Spanish, many of them being in our Hymnal. Our one original hymn from his pen is "How happy is the pilgrim's lot" (624), the rest, save for a quatrain doxology, being translations or alterations.

An important commentary upon the hymnodic inspirations of the Wesleyan movement in the eighteenth century is to be found in the remarkable list of hymn-writers in the Hymnal, who were allied with the Wesleys either in active work or frequent sympathetic communication. The Rev. Robert Seagrave (1693–1764), famous for "Rise, my soul, and stretch thy wings" (623), a clergyman of the Established Church, became a coworker with the Wesleys. The two Welshmen, the Rev. William Williams (1717–91), author of "Guide me, O thou great Jehovah" (91), and John Cennick (1718–55), author of three hymns—one of them, "Lo! He comes, with clouds descending" (601), being famed as the English "Dies Iræ"—were both active in the new evangelism. Cennick was a lay preacher. Their Calvinism, however, later led them apart from the Wesleys. Likewise the Rev. William Hammond (1719–83), at first a Calvinistic Methodist, finally joined the Moravians. The Rev. Thomas Olivers (1725–99), a cobbler converted under White-field, became a great Wesleyan preacher, and wrote "The God of Abraham praise" (4) and "O thou God of my salvation" (25). The familiar "All hail the power of Jesus' name" (180) was written by the Rev. Edward Perronet (1721?–1792), who for eight years was intimately associated with the Wesleys. The Rev. Robert Robinson (1735–90), author of "Come, thou Fount of every blessing" (19), and the Rev. John Fawcett (1740–1817), author of "Blest be the tie that binds" (556), and four other hymns of ours, were both converted under Whitefield's preaching and became Methodists, though the latter afterward served a Baptist church. So each one of these eight sacred poets drew spiritual inspiration from Methodism.

The author of "Rock of Ages" (279), the Rev. Augustus M. Toplady (1740–78), really belonged to the new evangelistic movement; but his Calvinism kept him in violent controversy with John Wesley. Before he was thirty years old he had received an ecclesiastical appointment in London, but his frail body and emotional temperament could not withstand the overwork and the onslaughts of the disease that conquered him within ten years.

The Rev. Joseph Hart (1712–68), who wrote "Come, ye sinners" (259), and three more of our hymns, was a Congregationalist. The Rev. Benjamin Beddome (1717–95), the Rev. Samuel Medley (1738–99), the Rev. Dr. Samuel Stennett (1727–95), and the Rev. Benjamin Francis (1734–99), each represented by three or four of our hymns, were Baptists. Stennett's grandfather, the Rev. Joseph Stennett (1663–1713), wrote our hymn, "Another six days' work is done" (70).

Sir Robert Grant (1785–1838), a member of Parliament and later governor of Bombay, and Reginald

Heber (1783–1826), Bishop of Calcutta, each wrote six of our hymns. Both were hymnodists of the first literary rank, both were deeply devout, both died in India. Bishop Heber, the more missionary of the two in spirit, is best known to us by the hymn: "From Greenland's icy mountains" (655); Sir Robert Grant by "O worship the King" (106).

The influences of the Oxford Movement in the early nineteenth century for the regeneration of the Church of England have left a permanent impress upon English hymns. The Rev. John Keble (1792–1866), author of our morning and evening hymns—"New every morning is the love" (42) and "Sun of my soul" (47)—and also of "Blest are the pure in heart"(360)—preached in Oxford the famous Assize Sermon in 1833, which Cardinal Newman declared to be the first impetus of the Oxford Movement. These hymns are taken from his famous poetical work, "The Christian Year," 1827 (the last of these three hymns being a cento), which sounded forth strong notes of warning to the languishing army of the Church.

Cardinal John H. Newman's (1801–90) "Lead, kindly Light, amid th' encircling gloom," was essentially a product and an expression of the unrest and consequent gloom of this period. His formal entrance into the Church of Rome in 1845 was quickly followed the next year by the secession of Dr. Frederick William Faber (1815–63) from the Church of England to Rome. Although all of Faber's hymns were written after that decision, the spirit of eleven of them is so broad that they are used in our own Methodist Hymnal, some with theological alterations, as "Faith of our fathers" (415), others without change, as "There's a wideness in God's mercy" (98). Matthew Bridges (1800–93), author of "Rise, glorious Conqueror, rise" (161), and "Crown him with many crowns" (179), also left the Church of England for Roman Catholicism.

Of the older clergymen, contemporary with the leaders of the Oxford Movement, though less active in controversy, were the Rev. Henry Francis Lyte (1793–1847), author of "Abide with me" (50), said to be the greatest hymn-writer of his period; the Rev. William H. Bathurst (1796–1877), author of "O for that flame of living fire" (187), each of whom wrote three of our hymns; the Rev. Thomas Kelley (1769–1855), whose hymns are all peculiarly majestic in tone, and the Rev. Christopher Wordsworth (1807–85), Bishop of Lincoln, author of "O day of rest and gladness" (68). Each of the last two wrote six of our hymns.

Of the younger clergymen of this period, the Rev. Dr. Horatius Bonar (1808–89) was the most popular, having written twelve of our hymns, such as "I lay my sins on Jesus" (488) and "I heard the voice of Jesus say" (304). His wife wrote our hymn No. 529. Dean H. H. Milman (1791–1868), of Saint Paul's, wrote "Ride on, ride on in majesty" (150), Dean Henry Alford (1810–71), of Canterbury, "Forward! be our watchword" (384) and three other hymns of ours, and Dean Arthur P. Stanley (1815–81), of Westminster, two hymns and one translation in our Hymnal.

Among our six hymns from Bishop William Walsham How (1823–97) the most popular is "O Jesus, thou art standing" (282), while many pronounce his "For all the saints" (430) the greatest hymn added to our collection by the recent revision.   The Rev. J. S. B. Monsell (1811–75), the Rev. Godfrey Thring (1823–1903), the Rev. Dr. Edward H. Bickersteth (1825–), author of "Peace, perfect peace" (528), the Rev. John Ellerton (1826–93), author of "Saviour, again to thy dear name" (38), and the Rev. Sabine Baring-Gould (1834–   ), author of "Onward, Christian soldiers!" (383) should all be added to the list of successful clerical hymnists of this period.   Three or four hymns from each of them are in our Hymnal.

Four distinguished knights are also counted among the hymn-writers of the nineteenth century: Sir Robert Grant, already mentioned; Sir John Bowring, LL.D. (1792–1872), a noted Unitarian scholar and governmental executive, once governor of Hongkong, on whose tombstone was inscribed the first line of his hymn, "In the cross of Christ I glory" (143); Sir Edward Denny (1796–1889), a member of the Plymouth Brethren; and the Rev. Sir Henry Williams Baker (1821–77), Vicar of Monkland.

From some of England's greatest poets we have chosen two or more hymns.   Sir Walter Scott's (1771–1832) "When Israel, of the Lord beloved" (95), based on the one hundred and fifth psalm, is introduced into his novel, "Ivanhoe," where it is sung by Rebecca, the Jewess, at the close of the day on which her trial occurred; and his free translation of "Dies Irae," "The day of wrath, that dreadful day" (603), occurs at the close of "The Lay of the Last Minstrel," wherein it is sung in Melrose Abbey. Thomas Moore's (1779–1852) "O Thou who driest the mourner's tear" (522) and "Come, ye disconsolate" (526) are a part of his "Sacred Songs," 1816. Alfred, Lord Tennyson (1809–92), has given to our hymnody "Strong Son of God, immortal Love" (139), "Late, late, so late!" (743) and "Sunset and evening star" (744); and Mrs. Elizabeth Barrett Browning (1806–61), "Since without Thee we do no good" (504) and "Of all the thoughts of God that are" (541).

American hymnody made its beginnings in the metrical Psalms, as we shall see in later paragraphs. Timothy Dwight (1752–1817), one of the most celebrated Psalm versifiers, also wrote several original hymns. Two other great names in early American psalmody, Oliver Holden (1765–1844) and Thomas Hastings (1784–1872), are celebrated both as hymnists and as composers. Altogether there are nine such names in our Hymnal listed both as composers and authors, attached to the music or words of twenty-nine of our hymns. Besides Holden and Hastings the others are Sir Henry William Baker, Frances Ridley Havergal, Martin Luther, the Rev. A. H. C. Malan, Georg Neumark, the Rev. John H. Stockton, and Caleb T. Winchester. Most of them were also editors of musical collections. In only four of the twenty-nine hymns is the composer and author the same person.

Eight names great in the annals of American poetry

are to be found among the authors of our hymns. William Cullen Bryant (1794–1878),author of "Thanatopsis," etc., wrote four hymns of the present Hymnal, just half the number in the 1878 Methodist Episcopal Hymnal, for which he wrote especially a Temperance Hymn now omitted.   Nathaniel Parker Willis (1807–67), whose poetry attained widespread though short-lived popularity in the middle of the last century, wrote hymn No. 660; and his brother, Richard Storrs Willis, wrote the music to our hymn, "It came upon the midnight clear" (110), by the Unitarian clergyman, Dr. Sears.   "There's a song in the air" (112) is by Dr. Josiah G. Holland (1819–81), author of "Katrina," and editor of Scribner's Magazine. The two greatest American men of letters among our hymn-writers are Oliver Wendell Holmes (1809–94) and John G. Whittier (1806–92).   Dr. Holmes's "Lord of all being" (82) and "O Love divine, that stooped to share" (457) both appeared in his famous volume, "The Professor at the Breakfast Table."   Mr. Whittier's seven hymns breathe the spirit of devout humility so characteristic of the Quaker poet, a humility evident even in the very first lines of the hymns: "We may not climb the heavenly steeps" (128), "It may not be our lot to wield "(398), "I bow my forehead in the dust" (472), "Dear Lord and Father of mankind, Forgive our feverish ways" (543).

Three younger famous literary men have each given to us one hymn: John Hay (1838–1905), Lincoln's private secretary and President McKinley's Secretary of State; Sidney Lanier (1842–81), the poet of the

South, whose pathetic music sings sadly through the lines, "Into the woods my Master went" (745); and Richard Watson Gilder (1844–1909), editor of the Century Magazine, the son of a Methodist minister.

Two American clergymen, whose names are less known in other forms of poetry, have come to be regarded as the greatest American hymn-writers: the Rev. Dr. Ray Palmer (1808–87) and the Rev. Dr. Samuel Francis Smith (1808–95). Each was born in the year 1808, and each is represented by four hymns in our Hymnal. "The morning light is breaking" (653) and "My country, 'tis of thee" (702), are by Dr. Smith, and "My faith looks up to thee" (334), by Dr. Palmer, the last two being in the same meter.

The Protestant Episcopalian Bishop of New Jersey, George Washington Doane (1799–1859), so named because he was born the same year when died the "Father of his Country," wrote three of our hymns, all of them well known: "Fling out the banner" (639), "Thou art the Way" (133), "Softly now the light of day" (53). His son, William Croswell Doane (1832–), first Bishop of Albany, wrote "Ancient of days" (76). Just as the English hymnologist, the Rev. Dr. John Julian (1834–), editor of the great "Dictionary of Hymnology," produced one of our best hymns (15), so also did the American hymnologist, the Rev. Dr. George Duffield, Jr. (1818–88), in "Stand up, stand up for Jesus!" (386). Three of our hymns came from the Unitarian clergyman, the Rev. Samuel Longfellow (1819–92), who was a brother of the poet Longfellow; one hymn each from the Rev. Dr. Charles F. Deems

I worship thee, O Holy Ghost,
  I love to worship thee;
My risen Lord for aye were lost,
  But for thy company.

I worship thee, O Holy Ghost,
  I love to worship thee;
I grieved thee long, alas! thou know'st
  It grieves me bitterly.

I worship thee, O Holy Ghost,
  I love to worship thee;
Thy patient love, at what a cost,
  At last it conquered me!

I worship thee, O Holy Ghost,
  I love to worship thee;
With thee each day is Pentecost,
  Each night a Nativity.

William F. Warren.

Autograph Copy of Dr. William F. Warren's Hymn,
"I Worship Thee, O Holy Ghost."

(1819–93), the Rev. Dr. Maltbie D. Babcock (1851–1901), both New York city pastors; the Rev. Dr. Henry M. Dexter (1821–90), editor of the Congregationalist; the Rev. Dr. J. E. Rankin (1828–1904), president of Howard University, Washington, D. C., who wrote "God be with you"; the Rev. Dr. J. H. Gilmore (1834–   ), professor in Rochester University, who wrote "He leadeth me"; Bishop Phillips Brooks (1835–93), of Boston; the Rev. Dr. Washington Gladden, the well-known author; and the Rev. Dr. Melancthon Woolsey Stryker (1851–   ), president of Hamilton College.

Of the Methodist authors still living, the Rev. Dr. William Fairfield Warren (1833–   ), dean of the School of Theology, Boston University, brother of Bishop Warren, and also Professor Caleb T. Winchester, of Wesleyan University, each wrote one hymn. The Rev. Dr. Frank Mason North, secretary of the New York City Church Extension and Missionary Society, and the Rev. Dr. Benjamin Copeland, pastor of the Humboldt Parkway Church, in Buffalo, New York, each wrote two hymns. Dr. North's beautiful lines were inspired by the crying needs of his missionary work in the city (423):

> Where cross the crowded ways of life,
>   Where sound the cries of race and clan,
> Above the noise of selfish strife,
>   We hear thy voice, O Son of man!

To which he adds in the fifth verse this plaintive prayer:

> O Master, from the mountain side,
>   Make haste to heal these hearts of pain,

> Among these restless throngs abide,
> O tread the city's streets again.

H. M. Chalfont has already calculated[1] that of 301 authors in the Methodist Hymnal about one half are clergymen and over one sixth are women. Fifty-three women have written eighty-seven hymns. Sixteen feminine names were dropped from the Methodist Episcopal Hymnal, and nineteen new ones added to the new Hymnal. While woman's work as a composer is relatively insignificant, comprising less than ten of our hymn tunes, her work as hymn-writer often reaches the height of spiritual sublimity.

The first group of women among the hymn-writers of the Methodist Hymnal consists of Mrs. Anna Letitia Barbauld (1743–1825), one of whose two hymns, "Come, said Jesus' sacred voice" (257), is a Methodist favorite; Miss Harriet Auber (1773–1825), a native of London and a devout member of the Church of England, whose missionary hymn, "Hasten, Lord, the glorious time" (637), is the best of our three hymns from her pen; "Mrs. Vokes," regarded by some as a *nom de plume*, author of "Soon may the last glad song arise" (630); and the greatest woman among hymn-writers, Miss Charlotte Elliott (1789–1871), author of five of our hymns, among them being "My God, my Father, while I stray" (521, 736) and "Just as I am" (272), probably the most powerful soul-winning hymn ever penned.

The most popular hymn by a woman is "Nearer, my God, to thee" (315), by Mrs. Sarah Flower Adams

---

[1] "Women in the New Hymnal," Christian Advocate, 1905, p. 1541.

(1805–48), a devout Unitarian, whose father, Benjamin Flower, was a political prisoner in jail for writing a defense of the French Revolution, when he met Miss Eliza Gould, who afterward married him and became the mother of Sarah Flower Adams.   With her hymn is sometimes compared another that is similar in spirit and meter, "More love to thee, O Christ" (317), by Mrs. Elizabeth Payson Prentiss (1818–78).

Miss Anna Letitia Waring (1820–   ), born in Wales, and Adelaide Ann Procter (1825–64), each composed three of our hymns, and Mrs. Cecil Francis Alexander (1823–95), in Ireland, two of our hymns, that may be classed among the very best.   They are all intensely personal in tone.   The first personal pronoun is used at least fourteen times in each of these hymns by Miss Waring, but always linked with the ideal of great humility.   The same thing is true of Miss Procter's three hymns, all of which are prayers for divine leadership, for divine blessing, or offering thanks.

Miss Frances Ridley Havergal (1836–79), to whom reference is made in the preceding chapter, wrote eight of our Methodist hymns, more than any other woman. Of Madame Guyon, Mrs. Browning, and the translators, Miss Jane Borthwick and Miss Catherine Winkworth, we have spoken elsewhere.

In our own land Mrs. Harriet Beecher Stowe (1811–96), author of "Uncle Tom's Cabin" and of the hymn "Still, still with Thee" (43), is the most famous woman in the Hymnal, though Mrs. Frances J. Van Alstyne (1820–), known as "Fanny Crosby," the blind poetess, has written more hymns than any other

woman—over five thousand in all.   Among Methodist
women should be named Miss Mary Artemisia Lath-
bury (1841–   ), whose Chautauqua hymns are in the
Hymnal, Mrs. F. K. Stratton (? –1910), and Mrs.
Caroline Laura Rice (1819–1899), wife of the Rev. Dr.
William Rice, of Springfield, Massachusetts, where he
was City Librarian until his death in 1897.

The Rev. Paul Weyand has shown that 258 of the
717 hymns of the Hymnal, or thirty-six per cent, were
written by ministers' children, sons and daughters.[1]
Of these it may be observed more than half came from
the zealous occupants of the Epworth Rectory, the
Wesleys.

THE TRANSLATIONS

Religious thought has coursed through many different languages since the Day of Pentecost, and while
there are many truths of Christianity that have found
their noblest expression in the English language, there
are but few doctrines that have not been at least
partially enunciated in some other language.   This
debt of ours to other tongues may be distinctly traced
in our hymnology; and, while it would be a colossal,
if not to some extent impossible, task to relate each
devotional idea in our hymns to its original source,
it is by no means impossible or uninteresting to seek
out the original hymns written in some other language,
from which many of the hymns we now use have been
translated into English, some of them freely and
some of them with great accuracy.

[1] "Ministers' Children as Authors in the New Hymnal," Christian Advocate (N. Y.), 1906, p. 721.

From the Danish hymn "Igjennem Nat og Traeng-sel," by the eminent poet and professor of the Danish language and literature at the Academy of Soro, Zealand, Denmark, Bernhardt S. Ingemann, has come our hymn (567), "Through the night of doubt and sorrow," translated by the Rev. Sabine Baring-Gould.

William Cowper's translation from the French of Madame Guyon's "Amour que mon âme est contente" has produced our hymn (518) "My Lord, how full of sweet content, I pass my years of banishment," and recalls, as has been previously stated, her persecution by the Church of Rome because of the faith that she held so dear. Another hymn from the French is Antoinette Bourignon's "Venez, Jesus, mon salu-taire," which John Wesley translated into our hymn (379), "Come, Saviour, Jesus, from above."

From the Hebrew was derived the hymn (4) "The God of Abraham praise," practically a translation by Thomas Olivers of the Hebrew Yigdal, or Doxology, which rehearses in metrical form the thirteen articles of the Hebrew creed. This was originally compiled by Daniel ben Judah, a mediæval writer, although the creed itself was compiled before this in the twelfth century by Moses Maimonides. The story is repeated concerning Thomas Olivers, a militant co-worker of John Wesley's, that he was first inspired to write this wonderful English version by hearing the Hebrew hymn sung in a London synagogue by the congregation, led by Rabbi Leoni, to the tune that in our Hymnal bears his name. The twelve verses, taken from Olivers's long poem, that made hymns 1075,

1076, and 1077 in the Methodist Episcopal Hymnal, have been compressed into one hymn of six verses in this Hymnal. The debt of our hymnology to the Hebrew language is very great through the metrical translation of the Scriptures. Undoubtedly some of these scriptural hymns were made from the King James English version of the Bible, though surely some give evidence of having come directly from the original Hebrew.

One of the earliest and most famous collections of metrical translations of the Psalms was the famous Sternhold and Hopkins book, published in London in 1562. Sternhold, in a sense the father of English psalmody, had died thirteen years before, but his work was brought to a certain perfection by the Oxonian poet, John Hopkins. This book was used for a hundred and thirty years until the Restoration. From it we get the hymn in the 1878 Hymnal, "The Lord descended from above." In Scotland the psalm books begin with the 1564 psalter, which was later supplanted by other books, as the "Royal Psalter" in 1630, and the famous "Rous' Version" in 1643, amended in 1650. But in England the Sternhold and Hopkins book was not supplanted until "The New Version," 1696, by two Irishmen, Nahum Tate (1652–1715) and the Rev. Nicholas Brady (1659–1726), met with widespread and lasting favor. As late as 1789 this book was adopted by the Protestant Episcopal Church in America. From this collection we get such well-known hymns as: "To Father, Son, and Holy Ghost," Doxology (720), "As pants the hart for cooling streams" (316), and "O Lord, our fathers oft have told" (700).

In 1707 Isaac Watts, in whom the metrical translation of the Psalms reached its highest beauty, produced "Imitations of the Psalms of David in the language of the New Testament." From this great work have come many of the fifty-three hymns from Watts's pen in the Methodist Hymnal.

In America the first psalm book printed was "The Bay Psalm Book," 1636, which replaced the "Ainsworth Version" from Holland, then in use. In 1785 Joel Barlow and in 1800 Timothy Dwight made important American revisions of the metrical psalms of Isaac Watts, and from the latter we have "I love thy kingdom, Lord" (208). Timothy Dwight also wrote, "While life prolongs its precious light" (254) and "Shall man, O God of light and life" (596).

While two centuries ago the Church regarded as little less than sacrilegious the singing in divine worship of other hymns than translations from the Scriptures, to-day the popularity of original hymns is fast crowding the ancient metrical psalm out of our hymnals. Three fifths of the metrical psalms in the old Methodist Episcopal Hymnal are not in the new Hymnal. Most of those omitted were by Watts, Wesley, and Montgomery, about equally divided between the three. Two from Milton, one from Tate and Brady, and one from Sternhold were among the banished. Of those metrical psalms retained from the old in the new Hymnal by far the largest number are by Isaac Watts, which argues the better adaptability of many of his translations, strong in thought and simple in vocabulary, to our modern taste.

Besides the Psalms, many other translations from the Hebrew Scriptures appear in our Hymnal, while the very free translations and hymns largely based on certain passages greatly outnumber the strict translations. Philip Doddridge scarcely ever wrote, save in following closely the Scriptural thought and phrase. Charles Wesley translated into hymns the language of Isaiah, Proverbs, Ezekiel, and Micah; and Newton and Cowper also verses from Isaiah.

While the New Testament has undoubtedly exerted the larger influence over modern hymnology, there have come from the New Testament Greek much fewer translations into hymns than from the Old Testament Hebrew. Some of the former are Watts's "Come, let us join our cheerful songs" (24), from Rev. 5. 11–13; Newton's "May the grace of Christ, our Saviour" (40), from 2 Cor. 13. 14; and Tate and Brady's "While shepherds watched their flocks" (115), from Luke 2. 8–14.

The venerable and scholarly Professor Harmon, of Dickinson College, used to delight in saying to his classes that if the angels in heaven choose some one human language in which to converse, it must be good, pure Attic Greek. Be that as it may, the noble Greek language produced for the Eastern Church some of the greatest hymns of the ages. They are marked by a strong simplicity of expression, combined in some instances with the most exalted devotion. Our hymn (672) "Shepherd of tender youth" was translated by the Rev. Dr. H. M. Dexter, a New England Congregational clergyman, from the earliest known Christian hymn: "Στομίον πώλων ἀδαῶν" (literally, "Bridle of steeds untamed"), by Saint Clement of Alexandria (A. D. 170–220).

Most of our Greek hymns are a part of that body of inspiring translations from the Greek with which Dr. J. M. Neale has enriched our English hymnody. The authorship of the Greek original of "Art thou weary" (293) has been a puzzling question for critics. Dr. Neale at first attributed it to Stephen, the Sabaite, nephew of Saint John of Damascus, though hymnologists have searched in vain for the original. Probably the clue to these difficulties is revealed in Dr. Neale's later comment that there was so little Greek in this hymn that it scarcely deserves to be classed as a translation. Indeed, while Dr. Neale's other translations in our Hymnal follow the original much more closely than does this hymn, his Greek hymns as a class have been regarded more as adaptations than translations. Dr. Neale's other Greek translations in the Hymnal are: "The day of resurrection" (164), from "'Αναστάσεως ἡμέρα," by Saint John of Damascus; "Come, ye faithful, raise the strain" (163), from "'Ασωμεν πάντες λαοί," also by Saint John of Damascus; and "Christian! dost thou see them?" (616), from "Οὐ γὰρ βλέπεις τοὺς ταράττοντας," by Saint Andrew, Archbishop of Crete (660–732). These last belong to a later period of Greek hymn-writing, which was distinguished from its predecessors by a marked difference in style.

Practically all of the hymns of the Western Church were written in the Latin, in which has been preserved the best thought of the Christian faith through at least the first fourteen centuries. The choicest of the Latin hymns were selected with great editorial care and embodied in the successive Breviaries, prepared under Papal supervision to standardize the various forms of worship of the Roman Catholic Church. These Breviaries contain not only the hymns but also the forms and ritual of the various offices to be used in the services of the Christian year. Julian mentions nine Breviaries: the Mozarabic (or Spanish), the Ambrosian, the Roman (from which Caswell largely selected his hymns in our Hymnal), the Sarum (in use in England before the Reformation, the chief source of Neale's translations), the York, the Aberdeen, the Paris (I. Williams, J. Chandler, and J. D. Chambers being the chief translators), the Hereford, and the Monastic Breviaries. Nearly all of our Methodist hymns from the Latin are translations from original hymns contained in one or more of these Breviaries.

Our hymn "All glory, laud, and honor" (31) is Dr. John M. Neale's translation of "Gloria, Laus et Honor," by Saint Theodulph of Orleans. Until the seventeenth century this hymn for Palm Sunday retained a quaint verse, of which the following is a translation:

> Be thou, O Lord, the Rider,
> And we the little ass,
> That to God's holy city
> Together we may pass.

Dr. Neale's two translations from the famous hymn

"Hora Novissima," by Bernard of Cluny, have attained great popularity. "Jerusalem the golden" (612) was taken from that part of "Hora Novissima" beginning "Urbs Syonaurea, Patria lactea;" and "For thee, O dear, dear country" (614), from the part beginning "O bona patria, lumina sobria." "Christ is made the sure Foundation" (662) is Dr. Neale's translation of that part of the hymn "Angularis Fundamentum" beginning "Urbs beata Hierusalem," the original authorship of which is still in doubt.

The greatest of all Latin hymns, "Dies Iræ," by Thomas of Celano, has inspired two of our hymns, "Day of wrath, O dreadful day" (599), by Dean Arthur P. Stanley, and "The day of wrath, that dreadful day" (603), by Sir Walter Scott, which are the most popular of the hundred and sixty English translations of this hymn that are known. Two fifths of these translations of "Dies Irae" were made in America; one man, A. Coles, wrote twelve of them. The most recent is "Day of ire, that direful day," from "Early Christian Hymns," by Judge Daniel J. Donahoe. While Dean Stanley's is a true translation, Sir Walter Scott's contains so much that is original in tone that it is regarded practically as an original hymn.

"Come, Holy Ghost, in love" is Dean Stanley's translation of "Veni, Sancte Spiritus," the authorship of which is sometimes attributed to King Robert II of France, although over this question hymnologists are still breaking lances.

"Creator, Spirit! by whose aid" (194) is a famous translation by the poet John Dryden from "Veni,

Creator Spiritus, Nantes tuorum visita," which tradition vaguely and probably incorrectly attributes to Charlemagne.

The most tender of all of our Latin hymns is the "Jesu, dulcis memoria," by Bernard of Clairvaux, which has inspired three of our present hymns, "Jesus, the very thought of thee" (533), translated by Edward M. Caswell, and "Jesus, thou Joy of loving hearts" (536), translated by Ray Palmer; the third (289) being treated upon a subsequent page among the hymns coming from the Latin through the German. The first of these two direct translations is widely used by English Methodists; but not the second. In fact, with this exception, all of the foregoing Latin translations have long been in use in the Wesleyan Church. Our Wesleyan brothers across the sea make use of Oakeley's translation of "Adeste fideles, læti triumphantes," while we use Caswell's translation, "O come, all ye faithful, triumphantly sing" (125). Over forty English translations of this hymn are known. None of the subsequent Latin translations here mentioned are in the new Wesleyan Methodist Hymn Book.

"Near the cross was Mary weeping" (154)[1] was translated by J. W. Alexander from the famous "Stabat Mater dolorosa," which has been set to music by many famous composers, such as Palestrina, Pergolesi, Haydn, Rossini, and Dvorak. The hymn is usually ascribed to Pope Innocent III (1216) on some-

---

[1] "The Latin Hymns of the Wesleyan Methodist Hymn Book," by Frederic W. Macdonald, London, 1899.

what dubious evidence; but was not authorized for public use until 1727 by Pope Benedict XIII. It is part of a larger poem in three divisions for use respectively in Vespers, Matins, and Lauds; and of the full text twenty-three translations are mentioned by Julian.

Of the history of the Latin chants in the Appendix to the Hymnal we shall not here pause to speak, though it is a subject full of interest to the scholar who wishes fully to acquaint himself with Roman hymnody.

Our beautiful hymn (483):

> My God, I love thee, not because
> I hope for heaven thereby,

is E. M. Caswell's translations of Saint Francis Xavier's "O Deus, ego amo Te; Nec amo Te ut salves me." Many believe that the Latin was founded upon Saint Theresa's Spanish hymn, "No me mueve, mi Dios, para quererte."

This flow of thought through several languages has produced many of our best hymns. Just as the last mentioned hymn came from the Spanish through Latin into English, so many of our hymns have come from the Latin through the German, and a few of these have had their source in a fourth language higher than the Latin, as the Greek or the Hebrew. The original "Gloria in Excelsis," for instance, was first uttered (probably in the Aramaic) by the angels that hovered over the hills of Bethlehem that first Christmas morning. At length it came to be written by the apostle in the Greek Testament, as in Luke 2. 14. This passage was expanded into an early Greek hymn of many verses, from which came the famous Latin version by Saint Theodulph (referred to above). From this the "Gloria in Excelsis" among the chants of our Hymnal is a direct translation in prose. Nicolaus Decius, in the sixteenth century, translated this into German from the Latin, thus: "Allein Gott in der Höh' sei Ehr" *et seq.* From this German version Catherine Winkworth has produced our hymn, "To God on high be thanks and praise" (93). A direct translation from the Scriptures of this first Christmas hymn is heard in Händel's "Messiah," to the triumphant music of the chorus, "Glory to God in the highest."

Likewise Anthony W. Boehm, at the beginning of the eighteenth century, made a German translation of "Jesu, dulcis memoria," which was the basis of our well-known hymn "Of Him, who did salvation bring" (289). Thus also came our lines "O sacred Head, now wounded" (151), translated by J. W. Alexander from the German "O Haupt voll Blut und Wunden," which, in turn, Paul Gerhardt had translated from the Latin of Bernard of Clairvaux, "Salve caput crumentatum."

The most famous of the German hymns is "Ein' feste Burg," written by Luther, who also composed the melody for this chorale. This was sung over Luther's grave at the Schloss-Kirche, Wittenberg. Our translation, "A mighty fortress is our God" (101), by Frederick H. Hedge, D.D., hardly outranks Thomas Carlyle's "A safe stronghold our God is still," of the

Wesleyan Methodist Hymn Book. Sixty-three translations of this hymn have been published. Another translation from Luther is our "Flung to the heedless winds," by John A. Messenger.

Nearly all of the principal English translators of the German hymns are represented in our Hymnal. From our standpoint at least, John Wesley is the most important of them all. Of the nineteen hymns in the Hymnal attributed to John Wesley, fourteen are translations from the German. Two of these are from the German hymns of Count Zinzendorf, the German mystic, "Jesus, thy blood and righteousness" (148), and "O thou, to whose all-searching sight" (359), the latter a free translation from "Seelen Bräutigam O du Gotteslamm." John Wesley also translated the following: "High on his everlasting throne" (221), a free translation of Augustus G. Spagenberg's "Der König ruht, und shauet doch"; "Shall I, for fear of feeble man" (225), from John J. Winkler's "Sollt ich aus Furcht vor Menschenkindern"; "My soul before thee prostrate lies," from the Rev. Dr. Christian F. Richter's " Hier legt mein Sinn sich vor dir nieder"; "Now I have found the ground wherein" (302), from Johann A. Rothe's "Ich habe nun den Grund gefunden"; "I thank thee, uncreated Sun" (367), from Johann A. Scheffler's "Ich will dich lieben, meine Stärke"; "Into thy gracious hands I fall" (305), a few verses of the hymn beginning, "Jesus, whose glory's streaming rays," from Wolfgang C. Dessler's " Mein Jesu, dein die Seraphinen."

Three of Paul Gerhardt's hymns were translated by

John Wesley: "Jesus, thy boundless love to me" (333), from "O Jesu Christ, mein schönes Licht"; "Commit thou all thy griefs" (435) and "Give to the winds thy fears" (437), both from "Befiehl due deine wege." Gerhardt's "O du allersüsste Freude" was translated into our "Holy Ghost, dispel our sadness" (192), by John C. Jacobi, assisted by the alterations of Toplady. Wesley's "I thirst, thou wounded Lamb of God" (335), was translated from two hymns, Zinzendorf's "Ach! mein verwundter Fürste" and J. Nitschmann's "Du blutiger Versühner." The complete cento included excerpts also from other hymns by Zinzendorf and Anna Nitschmann.

From Gerhard Tersteegen's "Verborgne Gottesliebe du" John Wesley wrote "Thou hidden love of God, whose height" (345); and from his "Gott rufet noch, sollt ich nicht endlich hören," Jane Borthwick wrote "God calling yet! shall I not hear?" (252.) She also translated B. Schmolck's "Mein Jesu, wie du wilst" into our exquisitely beautiful "My Jesus, as thou wilt" (524).

Catherine Winkworth's translations are recognized as among the most beautiful ever made into English hymns. Without deviating far from the German verbiage she preserves the strength and dignity of the original. Her seven translations in our Hymnal are but a small, though very choice, portion from her best work in this field. Her hymn, "Now thank we all our God," is but one of thirty translations by various authors from Martin Rinkart's "Nun danket alle Gott." Her other translations are: "Leave God to

order all thy ways" (476), from Georg Neumark's
"Wer nur den lieben Gott lasst walten"; "Whate'er
my God ordains is right" (487), from Samuel Rodigast's "Was Gott thut das ist wohlgethan, Es bleibt
gerecht sein Wille." Two of her translations are
from Petrus Herbert: "Now God be with us" (58),
from his "Die nacht is kommen darin wir ruhen
sollen," and "Faith is a living power from heaven"
(286), from "Der Glaub' ist ein lebendige kraft,"
which is a part of a larger hymn. Her " Fear not,
O little flock, the foe" (445) is from "Verzage nicht
du Häuflein klein," by Jacob Fabricus.

Carl J. P. Spitta's " O selig Haus, wo man dich auf
genommen" was translated by Mrs. Alexander into
"O happy home, where thou art loved the dearest"
(671); and Richard Massie wrote "I know no life
divided" (467), from a part of his German hymn,
which begins, "O Jesu, meine Sonne."

Matthias Claudius wrote "Im Anfang war's auf
Erden," which Miss Jane Campbell translated: "We
plow the fields and scatter" (716). The first line of
that most popular of all German Christmas carols,
"Stille Nacht," in our Hymnal is "Silent night!" (123)
though in many other hymnals it is "Holy night!"
From "Beim frühen Morgenlicht" Caswell wrote
"When morning gilds the skies" (32); from "Schön-
ster Herr Jesu" came "Fairest Lord Jesus" (118).

Nor does the relation of our hymns to foreign lan-
guages end with the catalogue we have just recited.
Many of these hymns have been translated from the
Greek and Latin and German into other foreign lan-

guages. Nearly all of Count Zinzendorf's best hymns, for instance, along with many other Moravian hymns, have been translated from the original German into Danish, Dutch, French, Swedish, Esthonian, Letonian, Wendish, and several other languages, besides the English.

But, what is of more interest to us, some of the best hymns originally framed in English have been translated into other tongues. "Take my life, and let it be" has been translated into French, German, Swedish, Russian, and several other languages of Europe and even of Africa. Its expression of humility has spared it from suffering the fate of the Russian translation of the gospel hymn, "Hold the fort, for I am coming," which was officially censored by the government of Russia as being too revolutionary in sentiment. A study of many mission hymnals, that we have examined, proves to us that we dare not attempt to sketch the linguistic fortunes of even one of the many international hymns, some of them passing into hundreds of alien languages and dialects on their errand of singing their great truths to the hearts of "every kindred, every tribe on this terrestrial ball."

As a class the most scholarly translations from the English have been those turned into Latin. For instance, several Latin translations have been made of the hymn, "The church's one foundation" (207), the best being "Nobis unum est fundamen," by the Rev. E. Marshall, 1882, and "Qui Ecclesiam instauravit," by T. G. Godfrey-Faussett, 1878. This hymn has been translated into all the dominant modern languages. The Latin version of "The King of love my Shepherd is" (136) that is best known is "Rex amoris, ut pastoris"; and of "When gathering clouds" (134), R. Bingham's "Quum circumcirca glomerantia nubilia cornam," wherein the sound of the Latin words seems to fit the rolling and rumbling of the clouds much better than the original English. The Rev. C. B. Pearson's translation of our hymn, " O come, and mourn with me awhile" (152) begins with the line, "Adeste fideles, mecum complorantes"—a startling contrast to the well-known " Adeste fideles, laeti triumphantes." Mr. Gladstone was fond of rendering into Latin as well as into Greek some of our best hymns. Our " Rock of Ages" he made into "Jesu, pro me perforatus," and our hymn, "Art thou weary" (293), he began with the line, "Scis, te lassum? scis languentam? " Macgill's translation of the same hymn begins, "Sisne lassus aerumnosus?"

The titles of the hymns are truly a part of the story of the hymns, though our interest in them is not so great as in the tune titles, since the former are not given in the Methodist Hymnal as they were in the Hymnal of 1878. Even in the older Hymnal it was the exception to find the same title to a hymn under which it originally appeared. The reason for this lies partly in the fact that some of the old titles were very long and unwieldy, partly in the taste of successive editors. For instance, originally our hymn "Author of faith" (298) was entitled, "The Life of Faith, Exemplified in the Eleventh Chapter of St.

Paul's Epistle to the Hebrews"; while "Make haste, O man, to live" (390) was entitled "Live." Both titles were altered for the reason just cited. Another long title is, "God's gracious approbation of a religious care of our families" (670).

The occasional caprice that has determined tune titles is not evident in the hymn titles.   The great majority of hymns derive their titles, like other poems, from the thought of the words. Some, however, in their title declare the occasion of their inspiration, as "For the Anniversary Day of One's Conversion" (1), "Written before Preaching at Portland" (241), "An Apology for my Twilight Rambles Addressed to a Lady" (498), "After Preaching to the Newcastle Colliers" (643), the stories of which have already been told in a previous chapter. The following original titles speak for themselves: "Comfort in God under the Removal of Ministers or other Useful Persons by Death" (592), "For the Dedication of an Organ, or for a Meeting of Choirs" (27), "A Liturgy for Missionary Meetings" (60), "The Holy Catholic Church: the Communion of Saints" (207), written by a Catholic on the Ninth Article of the Creed. Toplady's title to our hymn "Rock of Ages" (279), "A living and dying Prayer for the Holiest Believer in the World," was evidently intended for an answer to the doctrine that Christian perfection is attainable before death.

CHAPTER VI

THE THEOLOGY OF THE HYMNS

HYMNS are eloquent teachers of doctrine. Some hymnologists have carelessly stated that true hymns should not teach theology. The statement needs qualifying. Art best achieves her purposes when she least appears to be consciously striving for them. Likewise hymns are often the most effective teachers when they least seem to be didactic. The hymn-writer must assume the tone of prophet rather than logician, for syllogisms cannot be woven into the fabric of a hymn. Some of Isaac Watts's favorite hymns have been strangled by over-dogmatism. Nevertheless, the body of our hymns contains all of the fundamental thought on which our religious system is built; and there is not an essential doctrine of our faith that cannot be found in the Hymnal.

The influence of hymns as teachers of theology to the people can hardly be overestimated. Their very form is adapted to easy memorization. Clothed in language concise and chaste, swaying to the motion of rhythm, and rounded with rhyme, these poetical phrases that bear the great spiritual truths of the Church, when repeatedly sung to inspiring music, firmly fasten themselves upon the memories of the people.

William T. Stead, in his "Hymns that Have Helped," bears witness to the power of a hymn once deeply lodged in his memory: "It is Newton's hymn, which begins, 'Begone, unbelief.' I can remember my mother singing it when I was a tiny boy, barely able to see over the book-ledge in the minister's pew; and to this day, whenever I am in doleful dumps, and the stars in their courses appear to be fighting against me, that one doggerel verse comes back clear as a black-bird's note through the morning mist." An early American rhymed Psalter contains a quaint defense of the custom of setting the psalms to verse by insisting that verse is of lighter weight than the same bulk of prose, and therefore men find it easier to carry in their memories than prose.

Furthermore, the hymn and its melody from their very nature tend to be more often repeated, not only in church worship but also in the home circle and in private devotion, than is the formal statement of belief, or the exposition of theology from the pulpit. Our favorite hymns thus become a part of ourselves, and thereby give expression to principles which, from our inner experience and study of the Word, we recognize to be true, although often without having previously defined them clearly in our thought.

Martin Luther recognized this; and under his leadership hymn-singing attained its first widespread popularity among the people. With all Germany singing the hymns of justification by faith to the stately German chorales, the protest against the doctrines as well as the pernicious practices of Rome was given a mighty impetus.   Luther confessed that he won more converts by the use of hymns than by preaching.   Likewise the Wesleyan Revival made effective use of the hymns of personal religious experience, emphasizing the witness of the Spirit and the joyful assurance of acceptance.   To those who see the work of a Divine Providence through all the advances of history it appears to have been no accident that both Luther and the Wesleys, especially Charles, were *poets and musicians*.   Other men had recognized, and even preached, the same truths upon which the Reformation and the Wesleyan Revival were founded; but Luther and the Wesleys were given not only the power to preach and to organize the spread of these essential truths, but also the ability to express them in poetry and music.

In the selection of hymns there are two distinct tendencies that mark the work of the Hymnal Commission; firstly, the exclusion of hymns that are non-Methodistic in doctrine, and, secondly, the decrease in the proportion of credal hymns.

As to the first of these, let us inquire what are the non-Methodistic doctrines which find expression in hymn form.   Professor Warren, in classifying the theology of Methodism, admits of only four great distinct and complete Christo-theological systems, all others being incomplete or self-inconsistent.[1]   They are the Roman, the Calvinistic, the Lutheran, and the Wesleyan.   Their differences are based upon "the

[1] Cf. "Systematische Theologie," einheitlich behandelt, von Wm. F. Warren, Bremen, 1865, and "Centenary of American Methodism," by Abel Stevens, D.D., New York, 1865.

soteriological relations between God and man, as established by Christ."

The Romanists teach the salvation of a soul through the priestly power and the works of the Papal Church, introducing essentially pagan elements into their worship. Their faith has found noble expression in a wonderful body of hymns, most of them in the Latin. Their doctrinal hymns have, of course, not been admitted to any Protestant hymnal in their original form; but it is interesting to note that one of the most stirring war songs of modern Protestantism was written by a Roman Catholic poet, Dr. Faber, and is still sung by Romanists in its original form:

> Faith of our fathers! living still
> In spite of dungeon, fire, and sword.
> Oh! Ireland's heart beats high with joy,
> Whene'er they hear that glorious word.

The third verse begins thus:

> Faith of our fathers! Mary's prayers
> Shall keep our country fast to thee!

Calvinism teaches the salvation of a soul only through foreordination, or the free action of God, decreed before the foundation of the world. Against this dogma and its corollaries the early Methodist preaching hurled its most effective polemics. Accordingly, the Commission found itself under especial obligation to avoid those hymns which suggested the irresistible decrees of God, electing the souls of men to future life or future punishment without relation to character, and to admit in their stead those hymns which clearly teach the salvability of all souls accepting the salvation freely offered to all.

As a distinct reaction against the tenets of Calvinism have developed the doctrines of Universalism, teaching that all souls are to be ultimately saved; and of Unitarianism, which has added to this the denial of the triune nature of God, and the consequent divine nature of Christ, as the only begotten Son of the Father. The atonement conditional only upon its acceptance, and other doctrines dear to Methodists, were thus denied. In their anxiety to escape any suggestion of Unitarianism, the Commission took slight offense at the phrase addressing the Deity as "Eternal Soul" in Richard Watson Gilder's hymn (14), and Mr. Gilder, by vote of the Commission, was requested to change that phrase, which he naturally refused to do.

The exclusion of Calvinistic and Unitarian doctrines from the Hymnal has not fostered any prejudice against sacred poets of these faiths, as is attested by the great popularity throughout Methodism of the hymns, "In the cross of Christ I glory," by Sir John Bowring, and "Nearer, my God, to thee," by Sarah Flower Adams, both Unitarians, and also "Rock of Ages," by Augustus M. Toplady, the Calvinistic clergyman, who conducted such a bitter controversy with John Wesley.

Lutheran theology has made the salvation of the world largely dependent upon the proper use of the means of grace, the Word, and the sacraments, thus overemphasizing the forms of the Church and their

efficacy.   Methodism has not been obliged to combat
Lutheran doctrine so vigorously as Romanism and
Calvinism, partly because the latter two systems have
presented a greater contrast to the Wesleyan system
than the former, and partly because Methodism and
Lutheranism have not thrived so largely upon the
same soil.   Nevertheless, Methodist hymnology necessarily cannot teach the sufficiency of the means of
grace in themselves, but instead must present the
Church as a militant body of worshipers and witnesses,
the Word as a shining light illumining divine truth
(a figure employed in almost every hymn classed
under "The Holy Scriptures"), and the sacraments as
a means of expressing and stimulating Christian faith.
Neither attendance upon the church and its sacraments nor the reading of the Word in itself insures
salvation.   Our hymn (330)

> My hope is built on nothing less
> Than Jesus' blood and righteousness,

rebels against this teaching of salvation through the
means of grace.

In contrast to Romanism, Calvinism, and Lutheranism, the doctrine of Methodism, and, consequently, its
hymnody, has taught that the salvation of a soul
depends on "his own free action in respect to the
enlightenment, renewing, and sanctifying inworkings
of the Holy Spirit."   The phrase, Wesleyan doctrine,
is not to be taken as including all of the beliefs held by
the greatest Methodist hymn-writer, Charles Wesley;
for there are a few points wherein he differed from

his contemporaries and successors. Many of Charles Wesley's hymns were excluded from the Hymnal which would have commended themselves to the Church but for their undue emphasis of the "second blessing." The Commission was exceedingly cautious in admitting hymns upon sanctification that they might be thoroughly sound and orthodox. As a foil to rampant fanaticism on this subject, some of the Southern members of the Commission urged the omission from the Contents of the separate classification, "Entire Consecration and Perfect Love." But, since sanctification is clearly a sound Wesleyan doctrine, the Commission at length was content to admit twenty-eight hymns to this section, in which the Methodist Episcopal Church in the preceding Hymnal had used seventy, and the Methodist Episcopal Church, South, forty-five. Most of these twenty-eight express a yearning, a hope, a prayer for sanctification. Eighteen were written by Charles Wesley and three are translations by John Wesley. So modified is the expression of this doctrine under "Entire Consecration and Perfect Love," that this section raises the question as to the proper classification of some of the hymns. Nevertheless, our hymns have not slighted the orthodox doctrine of the Holy Spirit, as an illuminating, sin-dispelling, soul-warming influence, the Third Person of the Godhead.

Some hymns were brought to the attention of the Commission but not admitted to the Hymnal because of their teaching as to the second coming of Christ.

While Charles Wesley has hinted at this in his hymns, Methodism holds the belief that the Gospel through the Holy Spirit will conquer the world without the reincarnation of Christ. The Seventh-Day Adventists have transformed our Christmas Hymn into a hymn upon the second coming of Christ by singing it thus:

> " Joy to the world! the Lord *will* come,
> Let earth receive her King."

Likewise other classes of hymns were avoided, not so much because they involved questionable doctrine as because they offended delicacy, or genuine spontaneous spiritual emotion, or sincerity of thought. The sentimental hymn is excluded from the Hymnal and left for what the Preface styles as "those unauthorized publications that often teach what organized Methodism does not hold." Again, the hymns in the ancient style of dwelling upon the physical tortures of the lost are fortunately no longer in use, such as:

> Eternal plagues and heavy chains,
> Tormenting racks and fiery coals,
> And darts t' inflict immortal pains,
> Dipt in the blood of damnèd souls.

The overascetic tone of some of the older hymns has not been regarded as being in accord with the full, rich life which should belong to an active Christian. Hence Methodism sings no more the doleful verses beginning, "How vain are all things here below!" which Isaac Watts wrote in a fit of despondency, induced by a young woman's refusal of his offer of

marriage. John Newton's "Let worldly minds the
world pursue" is another of the many hymns dropped
from the preceding Hymnals for this reason.   Nor do
American Methodists longer sing as of yore Charles
Wesley's lines:

> Thou such mercy hast bestowed
> On me, the vilest reptile, me.

Modern taste revolts at the idea of a snake-like
humanity.

Literal references to the substitutional elements
have been avoided, which make too prominent the
physical side of Christ's death at the expense of the
deeper significance of his sacrifice.   These were the
chief doctrinal tests by which hymns were excluded,
besides the literary deficiencies, which, as will be
shown in the next chapter, caused the veto of most of
the excluded hymns.

The second tendency, distinctly traceable in the
work of the Hymnal Commission, is the decrease in the
relative number of credal hymns and the increase in
the proportion of the hymns of practical religious life.
Indeed, the whole trend of modern hymn-writing is
away from the ultra-dogmatism, exemplified by Isaac
Watts, and toward the expression of worship, devotion, and the joys of personal experience.   Christian
activity has been emphasized more than Christian
belief.

While on the negative side we have thus noted the
banishment of non-Methodistic doctrine and, indeed,
a decided decrease in the body of distinctly doctrinal
hymns, there is upon the positive side a statement of

practically all of the essential Wesleyan doctrines in our canons of sacred poetry.   In her early days, when bitter controversy was rife, Methodism was obliged to stoutly defend the theological tenets of John Wesley and his fellow-preachers against the contentions of opposing doctrines.   While the rationale of the Wesleyan theological system has not altered since it was uttered by John Wesley, the spirit of the Church has advanced and its vision has broadened, but always in a manner to confirm rather than discredit the logic of our original doctrines.   This can hardly be said of other evangelical denominations, whose creeds have suffered radical alteration.

In the opinion of many the most able statement in recent years of Methodist creed, contained within the small compass of three hundred words, is that uttered by Bishop Andrews in the Episcopal Address of 1900, and effectively quoted by Bishop Goodsell in the Episcopal Address of 1908.   Here, in concise and beautiful language, is presented the faith of Methodism, every phrase and almost every word being freighted with great meaning.   In order to show how fully our hymns coincide with our faith, we present in parallel columns each phrase of the creed and a line from some corresponding hymn, expressing the same thought.   The numbers in parenthesis refer to the hymn from which the line is quoted:

BISHOP ANDREWS'S CREED
We believe in one living and personal God,

THEOLOGY OF THE HYMNS
God is the name my soul adores,
The almighty Three, the eternal One (80).

Bishop Andrews's Creed	Theology of the Hymns
the Father Almighty, who in perfect wisdom,	No earthly father loves like thee (86). God is wisdom, God is love (88). The one Almighty Father (567).
holiness, and love pervades, sustains, and rules the world which he has made.	Perfect in power, in love, and purity (78). Thy voice produced the sea and spheres (80). Rules the bright worlds, and moves their frame (80).

We believe in Jesus Christ, his only Son our Lord,	True Son of the Father (125). O Lord and Master of us all (128).
in whom dwelt all the fullness of the Godhead bodily.	True Godhead Incarnate, Omnipotent Word (125).
who was in glory with the Father before all worlds;	Who from the Father's bosom came (148). Thou didst leave thy throne (122).
who became flesh and dwelt among us,	Pleased as man with men to appear (111).
the brightness of the glory of God and the express image of his person;	His head with radiant glories crowned (135) The Father's coeternal Son (153). Veiled in flesh the Godhead see (111).
who died for sin, the just for the unjust,	Bore all my sins upon the tree (153). And on his sinless soul Our sins in all their guilt were laid (155).
that he might bring man to God;	Is crucified for me and you, To bring us rebels back to God (153).

BISHOP ANDREWS'S CREED	THEOLOGY OF THE HYMNS
who rose from the dead;	Our Lord is risen from the dead (158). The Lord is risen indeed; The grave hath lost its prey (157).
who ascended on high,	Jesus, King of glory, is gone up on high (175).
having received all power in heaven and earth,	Jesus rules the world (177).
for the completion by grace and judgment of the kingdom of God.	The Lord Jehovah reigns, . . His truth confirms and seals the grace (81).
	Born to raise the sons of earth Born to give them second birth (111).

We believe in the Holy Ghost,	Come, Holy Ghost, our hearts inspire (181).
very and eternal God,	O Spirit of the living God! (188.)
by whose operation on men dead in trespasses and sin they are quickened to repentance, faith,	Thy Spirit can from dross refine, And melt and change this heart of mine (274).
	Whose Spirit breathes the active flame, Faith (298). Spirit of faith, come down (191).
and loving obedience;	Holy Spirit, . . . Reign supreme and reign alone (185).
are made aware of their sonship with God,	His Spirit answers to the blood, And tells me I am born of God (301).

Bishop Andrews's Creed	Theology of the Hymns
and are empowered to rise into the full stature of men in Jesus Christ.	Thy sanctifying Spirit . . . Make me pure from sin (378).

We believe in the impartial love of God to the whole human family,	And whosoever cometh I will not cast him out (295).
so that none are excluded from the benefits thereof,	And pledged the blood divine To ransom every soul of man (243).
except as they exclude themselves by willful unbelief and sin.	Will ye slight His grace, and die? (247.)

We believe that faith in Christ, the self-surrender of the soul to his government and grace, is the one condition upon which man is reconciled to God, is born again,	Give me the faith, that casts out sin, And purifies the heart (358). By faith I plunge me in this sea; Here is my hope, my joy, my rest (302). My God is reconciled! (301.) And tells me I am born of God (301).
becomes partaker of the Divine Nature and attains sanctification through his Spirit.	Rooted and fixed in God (375). Come, Holy Ghost, for thee I call . . . My steadfast soul, from falling free, Shall then no longer move (375).
We accept the moral law, confirmed and perfected by the Divine Teacher,	I read my duty in thy word; But in thy life the law appears, Drawn out in living characters (140).

BISHOP ANDREWS'S CREED	THEOLOGY OF THE HYMNS
and set forth authoritatively in the Holy Scriptures,	Thy word is everlasting truth; How pure is every page! That holy book shall guide . . . (204).
and we believe in the eternal consequences of good and evil inherent in the constitution of the human soul, and declared with the utmost solemnity by him, the final Judge of human life.	Assured if I my trust betray, I shall forever die (388). And bid his guilty conscience dread The death that never dies (245).

There are some lesser points of belief, or shades of meaning, in the Apostles' Creed that Bishop Andrews's creed does not specifically express, but which are clearly taught in our hymns. The Virgin Birth, for instance, is celebrated in hymns 111, 112, 117, 123, and 125. The resurrection of the body is taught in hymn 586, without prejudice upon the theological debate as to whether or not it is to be a physical or a spiritual body into which men shall be raised. In the following columns we have set corresponding hymns opposite some of the familiar phrases of the Apostles' Creed, not emphasized in Bishop Andrews's creed.

APOSTLES' CREED	THEOLOGY OF THE HYMNS
Christ, the only Son	Of the Father's Godhead true and only Son (166).
Suffered (under Pontius Pilate).	Pierced and nailed him to the tree (601).
Was crucified, dead and buried.	So Jesus slept: God's dying Son Passed through the grave, and blessed the bed (586).

APOSTLES' CREED	THEOLOGY OF THE HYMNS
The third day he rose.	'Tis thine own third morning, Rise, O buried Lord (166).
Sitteth on the right hand of God.	He sits at God's right hand (178).
From thence he shall come to judge the quick and the dead.	Christ is coming! (602.) Thou awful Judge of quick and dead (600).
The holy Catholic Church.	One holy Church, one army strong (209).
The Communion of saints.	O blest communion, fellowship divine! We feebly struggle, they in glory shine; Yet all are one in thee, for all are thine (430).
The forgiveness of sins.	Praise him, who pardons all our sin (20).
The resurrection of the body.	A glorious form Shall then ascend to meet the Lord (586).
Life everlasting.	All meet thee in the blessèd home above, ... Thy everlasting home of peace and love (671). In God's likeness, man awaking Knows the everlasting peace (160).

Thus all the main points of our theology are expressed in our hymns; and the great doctrines of the Methodist Episcopal Church are being chanted in the music of the sanctuary.

CHAPTER VII

THE LITERARY BEAUTIES OF THE HYMNS

REAL HYMNS, TRUE POEMS—LEGITIMATE EMOTIONS—
DICTION AND IMAGERY—RHYTHM AND METER

A RECENT work on hymnology proposes this statement: "A hymn is not necessarily a poem, while a poem that can be sung as a hymn is something more than a poem. Imagination makes poems; devotion makes hymns. There can be poetry without emotion, but a hymn never. A poem may argue; a hymn must not." This passage is based upon a false conception of the true nature of poetry. It is not difficult to carry to the inevitable false conclusion the proposition that not all sacred poems are hymns, even those cast in the usual hymn meters. But in order to prove that good hymns are not always poems one must assume an unworthy definition for hymns, as well as for poetry.

There can be no true poetry without emotion. One of the members of our Hymnal Commission, Dr. C. T. Winchester, professor of English literature in Wesleyan University, has treated of the emotional element in poetry in his work on literary criticism.[1] After quoting as representative of the modern conception the definitions of poetry uttered by Wordsworth, Shelley, Emerson, Browning, Leigh Hunt, Clarence Stedman, and Coleridge, all of whom recognized the

_____
[1] "The Elements of Literary Criticism," by Caleb T. Winchester, Litt.Doc.

emotional element as essential to poetry, he expresses the results of their thought in the following passage: "We may define poetry as *that variety of the literature of emotion which is written in metrical form.* Or, abandoning the strictly logical style of definition, we may say that poetry is that form of literature whose purpose is to appeal to the emotions, and which is written in metrical form."

A true hymn must be expressive of emotion, and somewhat in a universal sense, even though it be primarily the expression of a personal emotion. But this in itself is not enough. If the writer lack the ability or the inspiration for poetic expression, his most intense emotion may result in mere doggerel, as is too often the result. Such unpoetical rhymings, when uttering a great spiritual truth, may even produce a certain quality of emotion among the young or those who are ignorant in literary taste. As an example of the former, we find in William T. Stead's book, "Hymns that Have Helped," the following verses, which helped him most as a boy:

> His love in times past
>   Forbids me to think
> He'll leave me at last
>   In trouble to sink.
> Each sweet Ebenezer
>   I have in review
> Confirms his good pleasure
>   To help me quite through.

In spite of its bad rhyme and questionable logic, which his later tastes would condemn, these verses still recur to him with all of their helpful associations from his early days as a source of comfort to him now. The principle of association of ideas will psychologically explain the fondness that many of us bear toward some hymns, in themselves altogether unworthy of admiration. They are linked with stirring episodes in our lives, or else have held a very dear place in our hearts before the time when our minds were awakened to the real beauties of literature. But this peculiarly personal fondness for a poor hymn is no argument whatsoever for its use in public worship; and against this danger we must conscientiously guard. As for those who are unable or unwilling to recognize the emotional content of a hymn, and are constantly foisting upon congregations and religious assemblies the latest batch of doggerel, meaningless for the most part, and awaking only the emotions of ridicule or pity among thoughtful people, their case seems to be as hopeless as it is illogical. It is not enough that a hymn be wrought out of some intense emotional experience; it must have the power to reproduce emotion, and, from the very nature of a true hymn, its appeal to the emotions must be more or less universal.

When we add to this emotional quality the necessity of meter and rhythm, and these especially restricted to the most regular forms because of the demands of the music, we cannot escape the conclusion that good hymns must be poems. They form but a subdivision of that department of literature defined as sacred poetry. In general, it may be said that examples of nearly all the emotions expressed in other religious poetry may be found among the true hymns. But the most effective hymns avoid some of the emotions, upon which broader forms of sacred poetry may dwell with propriety. Wherein much sacred poetry differs from the hymns may be seen as this discussion unfolds.

Let us consider first the emotions which can be legitimately expressed by a hymn. In the first place, hymns may express the elemental emotions of either joy or grief. But in expressing or exciting grief through contemplation of the divine passion, through sorrow for sins, or through the suggestion of mourning for the dead, a hymn does not serve the highest emotional purpose in making grief a finality. It must at least direct the mind toward joy and its sources, such as our redemption through the cross, forgiveness of sins, and the higher meaning of sorrow and of the life beyond the grave. The following hymns are selected from many that beautifully illustrate the joyful purpose of a sorrowful hymn: "O sacred Head now wounded" (151), "Return, O wanderer, return" (255), "Weep not for a brother deceased" (594). Most Christian hymns may be said to be written throughout in the strain of profound joy; but where this joy is superficial and thoughtless, as in many a camp-meeting chorus, the effect is somatic rather than spiritual, and the reaction that follows is usually harmful.

Coming to the more complex and specialized forms of emotion, hymns may legitimately express such emotions as love, humility, sympathy, confidence or peace, and the feeling of social unity; but almost never their opposites—hatred, pride, scorn or ridicule, fear, and loneliness. In poems of wider scope, treat-

ing of sacred themes, as Milton's "Paradise Lost," and
Bickersteth's "Yesterday, To-day, and Forever," some
of these opposites may be portrayed in the course of
the narrative, though never as a dominant emotion.

Among the abstract sentiments hymnology expresses nearly the whole gamut of these emotions.
The feelings, arising respectively from the perception
of Truth, of Beauty, and of Right, may all be—indeed,
should all be—stirred simultaneously in the singing of
a hymn, each awakened by a different element of the
hymn. In so far as the intellect perceives that the
language of the hymn declares Truth, the pleasure of
the logical element is stirred. In so far as the poem
and its music appeal to our tastes as an artistic work of
real Beauty our æsthetic pleasure is stimulated. In so
far as we recognize the hymn as clearly pointing to us
the path of our personal duty our moral sentiments
are aroused. A defect in any one of these elements,
an error from truth, an inartistic expression in poetry
or music, a moral blemish in the thought, will at once
vitiate the effect of the whole hymn in proportion as
the defect is recognized; for, if any one of these sentiments is outraged, it will serve to create a sense of
incongruity, an emotional discord, that is fatal to the
very purpose of hymn-singing.

The sense of ridicule rather than devotion is aroused
by the incongruity of such lines as the ancient hymn
verse, known to some of our grandfathers:

> Ye monsters from the bubbling deep,
>   Your Master's praises spout;
> And from the sands ye coddlings peep,
>   And wag your tails about.

A generation that laid especial stress upon future eternal punishment produced this horrible verse, by Wigglesworth, on heathen and infant damnation:

> They wring their hands, their caitiff hands,
>   And gnash their teeth for terror,
> They cry, they roar for anguish sore,
>   And gnaw their tongues for horror.

This revolting picture, besides shocking the imagination, outrages our sense of truth and divine justice in consigning infants and heathen to suffer infinite torture because of the limitations of their age or environment.

Likewise those hymns that exhort to holiness for the sake of the rewards after death excite our contempt because, however beautiful they may be in other respects, they fall far short of the high ethical motives for holiness that Saint Francis Xavier expressed in the ancient hymn:

> My God, I love thee, not because
>   I hope for heaven thereby,
> Nor yet because, if I love not,
>   I must forever die.

In each of these examples of faulty hymns the emotional defect has made it impossible for use. A necessary condition for all literary excellence in poetry, and a necessary condition for the highest spiritual dynamics in hymn-singing, is the blending of all the emotions involved into a harmonious unity.

Professor George A. Coe in his psychological study, "The Spiritual Life," has uttered a forceful protest against the temperamental interpretation of the

Christian life, such as is too often presented by the Church. In a brief but valuable passage on "some psychological aspects of hymnology" he has shown how this one-sidedness is reflected in our hymns. Declaring that a difference in the quality of emotion is of much greater importance than a difference in intensity, he classifies the hymns according to their emotional attitude into two divisions. The first, by far the greatest in volume, represents the subjective attitude, the treatment of the religious life from the standpoint of personal experience, of introspection, of self-consciousness. The second, which by its paucity of expression seems to be greatly neglected, is the objective attitude, the expression of the religious life in practical activities, in good works, in Christian deeds.

His statistics, based upon the former Methodist Episcopal Hymnal, prove a better case than can be shown by the present Hymnal, for the Joint Hymnal Commission seems to have had his criticism somewhat in mind. We still find, however, that of the total number of hymns only 269 are under the heading of "Christian Activity and Zeal" (nearly one fifth more of the whole than the old Hymnal contained). The hymns of "Christian Activity" in the Methodist Episcopal Church, South, Hymnal appear to be in about the same proportion as in the Methodist Episcopal Hymnal examined by Professor Coe. Of the forty-seven hymns on "Christian Activity" in the old Methodist Episcopal Hymnal he found only nine treating "Activity" subjectively, directing the attention to the things to be done, to the activity itself; and thirty-two treating "Activity" subjectively from the standpoint of one's emotions during activity, while six were mixed or indeterminate.

Examples of objective treatment of "Activity" are: "Forward! be our watchword" (384), "Hark, the voice of Jesus calling" (402), the second verse of which was added in the new Hymnal to the two verses in both the old Hymnals:

> If you cannot cross the ocean,
>   And the heathen lands explore,
> You can find the heathen nearer,
>   You can help them at your door.
> If you cannot give your thousands,
>   You can give the widow's mite,
> And the least you give for Jesus
>   Will be precious in his sight.

Examples of subjective treatment of "Activity" are: "Am I a soldier of the cross" (393), dwelling upon blushes and fears and a study of the fighter's emotions rather than the activity itself: "Workman of God! O lose not heart" (392), and "Awake, our souls! away, our fears!" (405,) cheering against "trembling thought," mortal spirits that tire and faint, "native strength" that "shall melt away, and droop, and die."

It is not to be assumed that such hymns as these last, treating activity subjectively, are false in their emotion, or are undesirable in a hymn collection. Only the great disproportion between these and the other class of hymns on "Activity" itself is to be deplored.

We find that eight of the nine hymns in the old Methodist Episcopal Hymnal, treating "Activity"

objectively are included in the new Hymnal; and
most of the hymns treating "Activity" subjectively
have been dropped. Thus far there is a gain. But of
the seventeen new hymns under this heading only
three may be regarded as strictly objective. Sum-
ming up these statistics, we find that less than one
fifth of the hymns in the former book on "Activity"
are objective, but in the new Hymnal more than one
quarter.

In the old Hymnal the hymns dealing with any
kind of church work form less than half of those
classified under "The Church," in the new Hymnal
they form two thirds of the hymns on the subjects
formerly classified under "The Church." In the old
Hymnal the hymns on Christ's life and character
formed less than ten per cent of the body of hymns on
the subject of Christ; in the new Hymnal they form
over twenty per cent. Thus, in the objective treatment of "Christian Activity," "The Church," and the
life of Christ in the new Hymnal there has been a distinct gain. That it is an insufficient gain is partly
due to the scarcity of good objective hymns.

While it is true that emotion is a criterion of good
poetry, and, consequently, of good hymns, it is not
begging the question to say that the intensity, and to
some extent the quality, of the poetical emotion of a
hymn is often determined by the poet's choice of
words, for in the English language there are always
many different ways of expressing the same spiritual
truth. The legitimate vocabulary of hymns is greatly
circumscribed in both of two opposite directions. At

one extreme a great number of prosaic words, and a ·
still greater number of prosaic phrases, perfectly
legitimate in prose, are entirely out of place in poetry,
and, therefore, in hymns. Their commonplace nature
revolts against the art of hymnodic expression. At
the other extreme there is a wealth of poetic diction,
preciose words, ornate expressions, and elaborate,
fanciful figures of speech, perfectly allowable in most
poetry, but never in hymns. They dilute the spiritual
emotion of the hymn, or divert the thought of common
worship.

Our Hymnal is singularly free from either vulgar or
over-elaborate diction, because of the true literary
standards upon which the work of the Hymnal Commission is based. Nevertheless, within the limits of
good taste both simple and elaborate methods may be
observed in the literary style of our hymns. The
older hymn-writers preferred the former method.
Their hymns, that have survived to present-day use,
are marked by the simple, familiar English phraseology, such as in the German vernacular Martin Luther
commended and employed with great success. An
examination of Isaac Watts's hymns will illustrate to
the reader this simplicity of diction, in which most of
the old Psalm translations were made.

While Charles Wesley's vocabulary was much more
extended that Watts's, even within the same number
of hymns, it is largely confined to strong, simple words,
though nearly always in the best and purest English,
and in the less ambitious figures of speech.

The conscious self-restraint of these two foremost

hymn-writers of the eighteenth century is also to be observed in their contemporaries. This earlier school demonstrated that noble, majestic, thrilling hymns can be wrought out of simple words and figures. Possibly this may have given rise to the idea that hymns need not be poetic. Nevertheless, there is a true poetry in their austere chants that has stirred the spiritual emotions of many generations of men.

The modern hymn-writers, on the other hand, have greatly enlarged the vocabulary of hymnody, albeit within the bounds of propriety; and, furthermore, they have adopted a much wider range of imagery than their predecessors, who did not entirely scorn, however, the poetic figures of speech.

Our hymns abound in rich imagery. The doctrinal thought is intensified by an appeal to the imagination through the memory of all five senses. The sense of hearing is representatively awakened in the lines:

> Far, far away, like bells at evening pealing,
> The voice of Jesus sounds o'er land and sea (621);

of touch:

> Thy touch has still its ancient power (54);

> Jesus can make a dying-bed
> Feel soft as downy pillows are (Watts, 581);

of taste:

> His purposes will ripen fast,
> Unfolding every hour:
> The bud may have a bitter taste,
> But sweet will be the flower (96);

of smell:

> Our thoughts and thanks may rise
> As grateful incense to the skies (70);

of sight:

> Enthroned amid the radiant spheres,
> He glory like a garment wears;
> To form a robe of light divine,
> Ten thousand suns around him shine (23).

Through the vision of some bit of color the poet frequently portrays the deeper meaning of his thought. Thus we behold the royal richness of the coming of the morning:

> Still, still with thee, when purple morning breaketh (43);

> When morning gilds the skies (32).

Redemption through sorrow flames in the lines:

> His blood-red banner streams afar (416),

and

> I lay in dust life's glory dead,
> And from the ground there blossoms red
>   Life that shall endless be (481);

or the dazzling purity of the saints in heaven:

> Who are these arrayed in white
>   Brighter than the noon-day sun? (619.)

In the night scenes of the Hymnal our sacred poets have given to us some of the most beautiful imagery, that appeals to the sense of vision. What a picture Walter Scott has made of Israel's Divine Guide through the wilderness!—

> By day, along th' astonished lands,
>   The cloudy pillar glided slow;
> By night, Arabia's crimsoned sands
>   Returned the fiery column's glow (95).

The heavenly firmament by night, that inspired the
second verse of Addison's hymn,

> Soon as the evening shades prevail,
> The moon takes up the wondrous tale (84),

and Sir Robert Grant's hymn (203), employing the
selfsame imagery, gives beauty to the thought of these
lines:

Thou who hast sown the sky with stars, setting thy thoughts
in gold (714).

> Wait and worship, while the night
> Sets her evening lamps alight
> Through all the sky (57).

> He paints the wayside flower
> He lights the evening star (716).

Something of the wonder of night is deepened in the
poetic descriptions of the first Christmas night, as in
the old carol, "Silent Night," or J. G. Holland's poem,
"And the star rains its fire while the beautiful sing"
(112).   Contrasted with this stands the loneliness of
night:

> Cold mountains and the midnight air
> Witness the fervor of thy prayer (140),

and the symbolism of darkness:

> Thy tender mercies shall illume
> The midnight of the soul (446),

> Our midnight is thy smile withdrawn (82),

> Ashamed of Jesus! sooner far
> Let evening blush to own a star (443).

Charles Wesley's hymn, suggested by a night scene,
"See how great a flame aspires" (643), abounds in

imagery; but the figure is changed in each verse, and that which is represented by a fire in the first verse is symbolized by a shower in the last.

There is a startling vividness in some of the exquisite images in miniature:

> The lightning-rifts disclose his throne (686),

> The tumult of our life's wild restless sea (545),

> When trouble, like a gloomy cloud (539),

> The darksome prison-house of sin (654),

> Like some bright dream that comes unsought (537),

A long familiarity with old hymns sometimes dulls our appreciation of their imagery, as for instance Addison's biographical metaphor:

> When in the slippery paths of youth
> With heedless steps I ran (105),

and Sir John Bowring's thrilling lines:

> In the Cross of Christ I glory,
> Towering o'er the wrecks of time (143).

Much of the familiar, rich imagery of the Scriptures has been embodied in our hymns, adding to the beauty and strength of the thought. The Scriptures are represented as the "lamp of our feet" (205); the Eucharist, "Bread of heaven, wine of gladness" (235); aspiration, "As pants the hart for cooling streams" (316); and the Church,

> A mountain that shall fill the earth,
> A house not made with hands (214).

Nathaniel P. Willis draws from Holy Writ his picture of creation:

> The mountains in their places stood,
> The sea, the sky; and all was good;
> And when its first pure praises rang,
> The morning stars together sang (660).

Likewise Dr. Bickersteth's conception of life gives a biblical picture of the out-of-doors:

> Our years are like the shadows
>   On sunny hills that lie,
> Or grasses in the meadows
>   That blossom but to die (18).

As hymns are essentially reflective or hortatory, they afford little opportunity for the description of people, or personal episodes. But the few touches of this description in the Hymnal are drawn with vigor and beauty. It is true poetry that can flash such clear pictures in so few words as may be found in these lines:

> Where at sultry noon, thy Son
> Sat weary by the patriarch's well (12),

> When glory beamed from Moses' brow (187),

> In simple trust like theirs who heard,
>   Beside the Syrian sea
> The gracious calling of the Lord (543).

In the missionary hymns by a poetic touch of the imagination we are carried in a trice to distant lands. The realm of Mohammedanism is suggestively described thus:

> Where the lofty minaret
>   Gleams along the morning skies,
> Wave it till the crescent set,
>   And the Star of Jacob rise (640).

Within the compass of a few lines (655) Bishop Heber carries us to "Greenland's icy mountains," "India's coral strand," "Where Afric's sunny fountains roll down their golden sand," "many an ancient river," "many an ancient palm," the land where "spicy breezes" "blow soft o'er Ceylon's isle"; in fact, suggesting the whole earth, through which the gospel must be borne until "it spreads from pole to pole."

From the very limitations of hymnody there is little freedom offered for dramatic development. A few of the hymns suggest dialogue in their questions and answers. "Watchman, tell us of the night" (636) is a dialogue throughout, each couplet alternately being the words of either the Traveler or the Watchman. This is marked by the device of placing the first word of each two lines in the vocative. Thus, we read:

> Watchman, tell us of the night,
> What its signs of promise are,

to which the Watchman replies:

> Traveler, o'er yon mountain's height
> See that glory-beaming star!

Thus the conversation proceeds dramatically through the whole hymn.

Another hymn of questions and answers is the ancient Greek hymn (293):

> Art thou weary, art thou languid,
> Art thou sore distressed?

to which the reply comes with a flood of comfort and love:

> Come to me, saith One, and, coming,
> Be at rest.

Each verse of the hymn is patterned after this design.

In the Hymnal under the division "The Gospel," we find that the hymns sounding forth "The Need of Salvation" and "Warnings and Invitations" speak with dramatic emphasis. Eight of the first dozen hymns in this section ask startling questions to awaken the slumbering conscience.

Charles Wesley's great hymn, "Come, O thou Traveler unknown" is a thrilling drama in miniature; and, though the hymn utters the words of but one of the two wrestlers in that battle of love, the action throughout is intense, and the progress of the contest is followed at every step.

The metrical forms into which is molded the poetry of hymns are comparatively few. This is due to the limitations of the hymn tunes, their musical form, and the impossibility of repeating words and phrases, as in song form, except in the refrain. A few unusual meters creep into our hymnody, for which tunes must be especially constructed, sometimes successfully, as "Lead, kindly Light," or "Be strong!" (407), and sometimes not so successfully.

The stately hymn meters progress nearly always through lines of many syllables. Aside from the short meter poems (6. 6. 8. 6.), only a small percentage (less than eight per cent.) of the hymns begin with a line less than seven syllables, while the average line of the whole collection is nearly eight. The rhythm is also marked with stateliness and dignity, as befitting the subjects of hymnody. With the exceptions noted later in this chapter, our hymns are based almost entirely upon the two-beat rhythm, two syllables occurring in each foot of meter. This rhythm is distinctly recognized by authorities as fitting to the poetry of reflection, in contrast to the poetry of narrative and motion.[1]

On this two-beat rhythm are built our most popular metrical forms—common meter, long meter, and short meter. Long meter is uniformly made of eight-syllable lines, each containing four feet of two beats to each foot: ⌣ ́ | ⌣ ́ | ⌣ ́ | ⌣ ́ |
Of its various forms there are 114 examples, besides 7 with refrain added. Of common meter the first and third lines are of eight syllables each, as in long meter, but the second and fourth are of only six syllables. This is said to be the feeblest of the meters for general poetic use. Of its four, six, and eight-line verses there are 114 examples in the Hymnal.

⌣ ́ | ⌣ ́ | ⌣ ́ | ⌣ ́ |
⌣ ́ | ⌣ ́ | ⌣ ́ |

Short meter is so called because the syllables of each four-line verse are in the order of 6. 6. 8. 6.; and of these there are 36 examples, besides 8 with a refrain.

⌣ ́ | ⌣ ́ | ⌣ ́ |
⌣ ́ | ⌣ ́ | ⌣ ́ |
⌣ ́ | ⌣ ́ | ⌣ ́ | ⌣ ́ |
⌣ ́ | ⌣ ́ | ⌣ ́ |

It is to be regretted that in the Metrical Index the

[1] "The Musical Basis of Verse," by J. P. Dabney. Longmans, Green & Co., 1911, pp. 66 *et seq.*

full names of these three meters are not given, but
only their initial letters. The C. P. M., L. P. M. and
H. M. of the Methodist Episcopal Hymnal have,
fortunately, given place to the more definite terms,
8. 8. 6. Double, 8. 8. 8. Double and 6. 6. 6. 6. 8. 8. respectively. A brief study of the Metrical Index,
which, by the way, should be mastered by everyone
conducting worship regularly, will soon familiarize the
student with the metrical forms there enumerated.
The numbers at the top of each group refer to the
number of syllables in the successive lines, recurring
in regular order. For example, if you will count the
syllables in "Angel Voices," in hymn 27, you will find
that the lines of each verse arrange themselves in the
number of syllables they contain, as follows: 8. 5. 8. 5.
8. 4. 3., which is the heading under which the hymn
and tune are classed. The word "Double" and the
"s" pluralizing the number to which it is attached,
and the letter "l" for "lines," merely refer to the
number of lines, in which the number-schemes of the
syllables are repeated. With these few rules in mind,
a glance at the ninety-one different metrical forms
specified will satisfy one that there are not many
radical differences in meter.

The long, common, and short meters are closely
related, as we have seen. Now, when the weak
syllable is omitted from the long meter line, and the
stronger "direct attack" is made we get the 7s meter.
Sometimes alternate lines have feminine rhymes (or
double syllables that rhyme). Thus, about two thirds
of our 8s 7s hymns rhyme on the odd lines (double), as

well as on the even, as "In the cross of Christ I glory" (143), while the other one third end in an unrhyming double syllable. "The King of love my Shepherd is" (136) serves as a rare illustration of the feminine rhymes in the second and fourth lines of the stanza. Of this two-beat rhythm the noblest form is the 10s. Well suited to heroics, as well as to lofty religious thought, it is inappropriate for frivolous, dainty, or light expressions. Of slightly varying forms of this meter there are several illustrations in the Hymnal.

Besides the ninety-one meters enumerated in the Index, there is a double classification, P. M., called "Particular Meter" (or "Peculiar Meter," as some have it), and P. M. with Refrain, serving as a sort of wastebasket, into which an editor can throw all the meters that are left over. For this reason it should have been placed at the very end of the Metrical Index, as in the Hutchins, Parker, Tucker, and other hymnals. The purpose of a metrical index is to enable a pastor or choirmaster to quickly choose for any given hymn a different tune from the one to which it is set, but of the same meter. For this particular purpose the P. M. group is utterly useless, and it is surprising that no hymnal has ever labeled the P. M. wastebasket as useless in that respect, warning us that hymns under this heading, far from being all of the same meter, are, in fact, none of them of the same meter.

Besides the inaccuracies in the Metrical Index, some of its classifications are misleading. In this respect, it is true, our Hymnal is following the bad precedent set by most of the best hymnals, which should some day be overruled. But, who, for instance, cares to sing "Sweet hour of prayer" to the tune "Contrast"? They have the same number of syllables, and are both classed as "8s Double"; but the hymn is a double rhythm and the tune is a triple rhythm. Who would sing Kipling's "Recessional" to the 8. 8. 8. Double tune "Nashville," even though they are both classed as "8s 6 lines"; or "Welcome, happy morning!" to the tunes of "The Lord is my Shepherd"; or "Come unto me when shadows" to the tune of "True-hearted, whole-hearted"; or "Long years ago o'er Bethlehem's hill" to the tune "Bethlehem"? And yet each one of these couples is grouped under the one metrical heading, thus defeating the very purpose of the Metrical Index.

Apropos of this last tune, beware of the "Irregulars" in this Index! Except for the word "Mary," Phillips Brooks's poem, to which our tunes "Bethlehem" and "Saint Louis" are set, is clearly a 8. 6. 8. 6. 7. 6. 8. 6. hymn; and is not 8s 6s Double. The other tunes under this heading have a refrain. "Amsterdam" is not irregular, but is a regular 7. 6. 7. 6. 7. 7. 7. 6. tune. And "Epiphany" deserves only the awkward metrical title "10. 11. 11. 11. 12. 11. 10. 11"; but is regular according to that scheme.

As for hymns with refrains, both "Paradise" tunes use refrains, as do also five of the plain P. M. tunes, although "Beyond" is classed under " P. M. with Refrain." It might be advisable for a hymnal using a score of hymns with refrains to group these together under a note that they are not interchangeable, instead of making nearly as many separate metrical headings.

There is a class of genuinely irregular tunes to be found among the nondescripts of P. M. Every verse of the regular meters conforms to a given scheme; but the verses of the irregular forms are mutually incon sistent, and to guide the singer the notes of the music must be tied, using in some verses, but not in others, one note to each syllable. This we see in the tune "Elliott." But in singing the words of the hymn, "Thou didst leave thy throne," a congregation is very apt to become confused as to which syllables are to be sung to the tied notes. As it is written, there are two ways of singing either the first or the second lines of the last verse; and the usual confusion at this point sometimes not only confuses a congregation but inevitably drives them to a painfully false accent. The tune "Cary" fits well the first verse of "One sweetly solemn thought," but compels us to accent the ultimate of each bisyllabic word in the last lines of the third verse with ludicrous effect:

> Near-er' leav-ing' the cross,
> Near-er' gain-ing' the crown.

This fault is intrinsic in the irregularity of the poetical meter, although R. S. Ambrose's famous melody to these words avoids this difficulty somewhat. These irregularities but emphasize the fact that hymn meters should be confined to strict limitations, and to be successful must easily yield to regular scansion, each foot containing the same number of syllables as the corresponding feet in other verses.

While meter and emotional expression are essential to poetry, the meter must always be subordinate to the emotion. To inquire into the emotional fitness of certain meters among our hymns would lead us too far afield. Let one illustration suffice to mark the principle—the appropriateness of the more active three-beat rhythm to joyous themes. There are but few poems in the Hymnal using the three-beat rhythm. The twenty hymns whose meter is composed of the various combinations of 6s and 4s are all reducible to triple rhythm, such as "America" and "More love to thee, O Christ." About one third of the remaining hymns of this rhythm are to be found in the group of hymns expressing the joy of Christmas time, as "There's a song in the air," which sustains the triple beat throughout; "In the field with their flocks abiding"; and "Silent Night," which bears only a gentle suggestion of this rhythm. Nearly all of the other triple-beat hymns in the Hymnal express a joyous theme in this joyous rhythm, as "O how happy are they," "True-hearted, whole-hearted," "Lift your glad voices," "Come, let us anew our journey pursue," "O thou, in whose presence my soul takes delight."

Thus emotion and rhythm conspire to make beautiful the poetry of our Hymnal.

PART III
THE TUNES

CHAPTER VIII

THE STORY OF THE TUNES AND THEIR COMPOSERS

<small>EARLY MUSICAL HISTORY—CONTINENTAL COMPOSERS—BRIT-
ISH COMPOSERS—AMERICAN COMPOSERS—NEW TUNES—
RELATION OF SOME HYMN TUNES TO LARGER FORMS.</small>

THE story of the hymn tunes has not been told so fully as the story of the hymns, save as it has appeared incidental to the general history of music. Hymnology has called forth hundreds of volumes to tell its story, while the history of the tunes can claim but comparatively few. Nor is this to be marveled at, when it is considered that hymn-writing is ancient, but music and, consequently, hymn-tune writing in its developed form is distinctly a modern art.

During many centuries in Europe the history of music was simply the history of church music. This was largely true also of early American music, which made its first progress through anthems and hymn tunes, just as our earliest government itself followed ecclesiastical principles. The Methodist Hymnal contains melodies from nearly every important period and school of hymn-tune writing, as we shall see in the illustrations that follow.

Pope Gregory (A. D. 590) placed the imprint of his genius upon the crude musical system of his day by adding new scales or modes to those that had already been devised by Saint Ambrose, and by reducing the

whole to a more logical system. As a result, the
Gregorian tones have ever since been the foundation
of the Roman Catholic Church music.   Of this ancient
Gregorian plain-song the Methodist Hymnal contains
little else besides a chant drawn from one of the
Gregorian tones, "Nunc Dimittis" (733) and a hymn
tune "Olmutz" (227), arranged from the Gregorian by
Lowell Mason. The old Latin melody (477), based
upon five adjacent tones, was probably derived from
the Gregorian music.   These melodies, now clothed in
modern harmony and rounded with a modern cadence,
were originally sung only in unison, like all the music
of this early homophonic era.   The popular idea that
the melody "Crusader's Hymn" belongs to this period
is incorrect.

By the innovations of Hucbald in the tenth century,
and Guido of Arezzo a century later, both of them
pious monks, sacred words came to be sung upon two
notes at the same time, instead of only one as before,
and from this the harmony developed through
successive centuries into an elaborate polyphony
(πολύ + φῶνος, having "many tones"), until it was
simplified and perfected by the genius of Palestrina
(1524–94). The Palestrina mass is still the model
of beauty in the worship of the Roman Catholic
Church throughout the world.

Until the Reformation, church music was entirely
in the hands of the clergy and their trained musicians.
It was left to Martin Luther, assisted by the musician
Walther, to bring worship song to the people themselves by means of the German chorale, simple in

melody, strong in harmony, and set to the familiar words of the vernacular, instead of the Latin. Hymn-singing had already been employed to a limited degree among the Bohemian Brethren and other sects; but now it became universal throughout the Reformed Church. This may be regarded as the beginning of the modern hymn tune.

Among the oldest examples of the German chorale in the Hymnal are "Ein' Feste Burg" (101), ascribed to Martin Luther; "Munich" (151), rearranged by Mendelssohn from an old chorale; the "Passion Cho-rale" (151) of Hans Leo Hassler and the chorale of Nicolaus Decius, of which we have two arrangements, "Decius" (93) and "St. Peter" (97). The German com-posers of the seventeenth century followed the same general style of chorale writing in "Nuremberg" (103), by Johann Rudolf Ahle (1625-73); "Nun Danket" (30), by Johann Crüger (1598-1662); "Bremen" (476), by Georg Neumark (1621-81); and "St. Theodulph" (31), by Melchior Teschner (about 1613). By playing these tunes, even amateur musicians can easily recog-nize the elements common to the German chorales, distinguishing them from the work of other schools, by a dignity of movement and a Doric simplicity of harmony, expressing a calm but lofty state of re-ligious feeling. No frivolous verses can well be sung to these stately measures, no thought can be appro-priate, save that which finds deep root in the soul life.

Later composers have given to us genuine chorales of great worth, though in their day already observing the beginnings of a different type of hymn tune. The

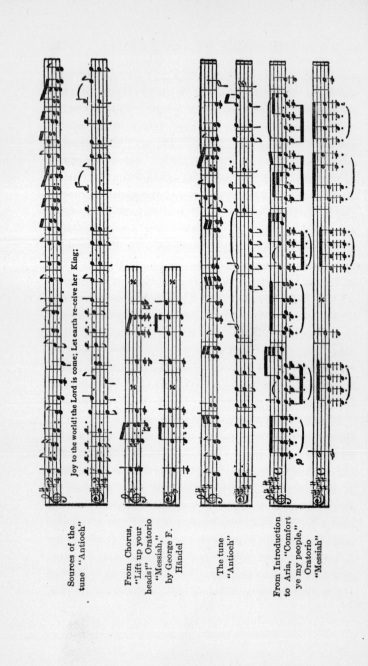

Sources of the tune "Antioch"

Joy to the world! the Lord is come; Let earth re-ceive her King:

From Chorus, "Lift up your heads!" Oratorio "Messiah," by George F. Händel

The tune "Antioch"

From Introduction to Aria, "Comfort ye my people," Oratorio "Messiah"

most recent of these, Arne Oldberg, a living American composer, has written for the Methodist Hymnal in the chorale style an excellent hymn tune, "Gilder" (14).

The great composer Händel (1685–1759) was a master in writing the chorale.   The six hymn tunes in our collection from his pen, however, were not written as chorales, but are melodies taken from his larger works (see end of this chapter), rearranged in harmony, and in some cases so changed in melody that we could scarce expect the composer himself to recognize them. The great German master musicians, beginning with Beethoven, in many respects the greatest of them all, on through the brilliant leaders of the later romantic school, have been levied upon generously for our hymn tunes.   We thus make use of eight melodies from Beethoven, four from Spohr, six from Mendelssohn, four from Haydn, three from Weber, two from Schumann, and two from Mozart, some of which have been traced in later paragraphs of this chapter to their original sources.

France and Geneva played an important part in the hymn tunes of the sixteenth century.   Of these we have "Old Hundred" (16), a melody that has reached the widest influence.   Its authorship is unknown. It is supposed, however, to have been adapted to Beza's version of the one hundred and thirty-fourth psalm for the Genevan Psalter, 1551, from a popular melody sung in France to the words, "Il n'y a icy celluy qui n'ai sa belle," and in Holland to the words, "Ik had een boelken intercorem, die ik met Harten minne."   The tune "Flemming" (478) was also taken from the Genevan Psalter, but its composer, Friedrich F. Flemming (1778–1813), was a native of Neuhausen, Saxony. Its resemblance to Webbe's "Glorious Apollo" has been noted by critics, though rarely provoking the charge of plagiarism. From Johann Georg Naegeli (1768–1836), who was born and died in Zürich, Switzerland, were taken "Dennis" (100) and "Naomi" (277). The former appears three times in the Hymnal, the latter four times.

Jean Jacques Rousseau (1712–1778) was born in Geneva, but through his brilliant work in Paris, beginning at the age of twenty-nine, his radical writings on music and his vigorous defense of the principles of the French Revolution, France may justly claim him and his music, from which we derive our popular melody "Greenville" (39). Of later French tunes, characterized by a charming sweetness of melody, we have the following examples: "Morning Hymn" (44), by François Hippolyte Barthélémon (1741–1808); "Gilead" (202), by Etienne Henri Mehul (1763–1817); "Rutherford" (614), by Crétien D'Urhan (1788–1845); "Messiah" (348), by Louis Joseph Ferdinand Herold (1791–1833); "Radiant Morn" (566), "Olney" (696), and a chant (738), by Charles François Gounod (1818–93), one of the great names in the history of music.

From England has come by far the largest proportion of our hymn tunes. Thomas Tallis, or Tallys, the father of English Cathedral music, was born some time in the second decade of the sixteenth century and died in 1585. He was one of the greatest musicians of his age, and in England indisputably the greatest. His

most valuable legacy to succeeding ages was the per-
fecting of the English hymn tune. The most famous
of these from his pen is in our collection and bears the
name "Evening Hymn" (49), though elsewhere it is
more often known as "Tallis's Canon." By a slow
rhythm, a most effective contrapuntal harmony, and
an easily flowing melody he has combined solemn
grandeur with delicate beauty. Its form as a canon
may be observed by playing the tenor part beginning
with the fifth note, from which point the tenor sings
the very same melody that was sung by the soprano
one measure previous, thus:

The immediate successors of Tallis made little advance in the art of hymn tunes; and their work in the Methodist Hymnal is found only among the chants, No. 729, by Henry Lawes (1595–1662), No. 728, by Pelham Humphrey (1647–74), No. 732, by Thomas Purcell, the greatest English musician of the seventeenth century (1623?–1682), and three chants, 730 and 732, by Henry Aldrich (1647–1710). The one exception to this is the hymn tune "Winchester Old" (181) by George Kirbye (–1634).

The English composers of the eighteenth century, especially those of the first fifty years, are represented in our Hymnal by stalwart tunes of optimistic melodies and strong radical harmonies. To recognize this the student has but to examine "Hanover" (11) and the great "St. Ann" (214) by William Croft (1678–1727); "Marlow" (8), by John Chetham (1685?–1760); "All Saints" (215), by William Knapp (1698–1768), and "Arlington" (354) by Thomas A. Arne (1710–78). The famous Henry Carey (1685–1743), to whom is attributed our "America" (702), belongs to this period. J. Christopher Smith, Handel's secretary, attributes also to Carey the original words of this tune, "God save our gracious King," as it was first sung in 1740 at a dinner to celebrate the capture of Portobello. Questioning Carey's title as composer of the tune, successive critics have traced it to an "Ayre" by Dr. Jan Bull, 1619; a Scotch carol, "Remember, O thou man," in Ravenscroft's "Melismata," 1611; a ballad of 1669, "Franklin is fled away"; and a tune by Henry Purcell for harpsichord or spinnet, 1696.

Nevertheless, many editors still give the credit to Carey. The tune was adopted as the Prussian national tune, and is also used patriotically in Denmark.

English hymn-singing fell to a low ebb during the middle decades of the eighteenth century. The Church of England seemed to be indifferent to the musical demands of worship. The production of hymn tunes became weakly imitative. Congregational singing languished. Though contemporaries were loath to admit it, there is no question but that the vigorous musical program of the Wesleys and its popularity among the people at large produced indirectly a marked improvement in the musical interest within the Established Church. From the work of the later eighteenth century English composers we have a dozen examples, the best of which are "Duke Street" (5), "Mornington" (45), "Truro" (7), "St. Stephen" (86), "St. Martin's" (183), and "Amsterdam" (623). In contrast to the earlier tunes of the century, one observes in these later melodies a much greater variety of musical rhythm and a more frequent use of two or more notes to one syllable, which gave greater elasticity but less solidity to the melody. The multiplying of many notes to a syllable was often

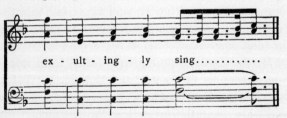

ex - ult - ing - ly   sing.............

carried in this era to a ridiculous extreme. A faint suggestion of this is found in two measures of the tune "Avison" (119), which bears the name of its composer (circ. 1710-70).

The tune "Miller" (17), usually known as "Rocking-ham," and sometimes as "Caton," was adapted by Dr. Edward Miller (1731-1807) from an older tune, "Tun-bridge." His psalm books sounded the knell of the old style psalm tune by popularizing better and more modern melodies.

Scotland's musical contribution has been made through psalm tunes. The first Scotch psalter (1564) was largely based upon tunes brought from Geneva and France by returning exiles. The most famous Scotch psalter, musically speaking, was prepared by Andro Hart in 1615, and from this we get our tune "Dundee" (96). Its old title, "French," and its majestic movement suggest a continental origin. Robert Burns refers to it in "The Cotter's Saturday Night":

Perhaps Dundee's wild, warbling measures rise.

"Caledonia" (385), the stirring war song mentioned in another chapter, has also come to us from Scotland.

Not only Scotland but Ireland also has had a part in the making of British hymn music, as some of the composers classed as English were born in Ireland, notably the Earl of Mornington (1735-81), Sir Robert Prescott Stewart (1825-94), and William V. Wallace (1814-1865). Few composers have had a more world-wide romantic career than Wallace, who wrote

"Serenity" (128), "We may not climb the heavenly steeps." After a brief musical life in Ireland he wandered through the wilds of Australia, escaping death from the savages only by the intervention of the chieftain's daughter, and at last winning crude musical honors there. For one concert he was paid a hundred sheep. In the East Indies he played before the Queen of Oude. From Valparaiso, South America, he crossed the Andes to Buenos Ayres. At Santiago game cocks were the price of admission to his concert. Audiences in the United States and England were captivated by his playing, and soon he found English publishers for his operas and other compositions, which for the time became very popular. He died in the Pyrenees.

The Welsh people, with their passionate love of music and rare natural excellence in singing, have produced many wonderful hymn-melodies. The Methodist Hymn Book of England has preserved some of the best of these; but not so our American Hymnal, probably because their wild flavor is ill suited to either our popular taste or our musical traditions.

Among the English composers of the nineteenth century the writing of hymn tunes attained the highest excellence. A distinctive style of tune-writing was developed from the beginning of the century through the first four or five decades. In the latter half of the century, however, by far the largest proportion of the hymn tunes of the English school appeared, and at present they represent the most popular type of tune among cultured musicians and

authoritative hymn-book makers.   For the best
musical results the English tune must be sung faster
than the German chorale, or even the Scotch psalm
tune.   This may be explained partly by the fact that
they were written largely by organists, who were
accustomed to play hymns faster than their ancestors.
On the other hand, they are ruined by such a giddy
tempo as that which is necessary for the decadent
revival melody with chorus, which has thrived con-
temporaneously with the modern English tunes.
Four-four time with even quarter notes (or half notes
in the English books) characterizes a large proportion
of these tunes, though many of them display a remarkable variety in rhythm (as "Lux Benigna").

Of the earlier nineteenth century composers of this
school the most prominent represented in our Hymnal
were   Edward Hodges (1796–1867), one of our tunes
by him being "Habakkuk" (368, etc.); Henry John
Gauntlett (1806–76), whose three different tunes in
the Hymnal are not so popular as many others that he
wrote; James Turle (1802–82), who wrote "St. John's,
Westminster" (550), "Westminster" (700), and a
chant (733), all marked by a strong style of harmony
and an unusual succession of chords; and Samuel
Sebastian Wesley (1810–76), the grandson of the great
Charles Wesley, "Aurelia" being the best known of our
tunes by him.   The Wesley family contained many
able musicians.   Charles Wesley was the most profi-
cient among those at Epworth Rectory.   His two
sons, Charles and Samuel, attained a considerable emi-
nence in the musical world.   The latter was a prolific

composer. His eldest son, the Rev. Dr. Charles Wesley, edited an anthem collection, and his third son, Samuel Sebastian (referred to above), became the greatest composer and for a time the best organist in the Church of England.

There were five great leaders of the modern English school, whose names attached to hymn tunes are nearly always a guarantee of unusual excellence. They are (in the order of their birth) Smart, Dykes, Barnby, Stainer, and Sullivan. These men were all active in varied fields of English music, but in the realm of church music worked toward a common end, the production of hymn tunes that would meet the popular taste without sacrificing a high standard of excellence. Henry (Thomas) Smart (1813–79) wrote cantatas, part-songs, and compositions for the organ, of which instrument he was a master player. His blindness in 1864 was a serious handicap, but did not keep him from composing. His tunes possess charming melody and effective harmonic treatment. The Rev. John Bacchus Dykes (1823–76), the Vicar of Saint Oswald, Durham, was noted as a theologian and a musician. His distinction lies in his wonderful ability to express the spirit and thought of the hymn in its tune, although Grove refers slightingly to his "rather sentimental style of harmonization." He and Lowell Mason are exceeded only by Barnby in the number of hymn tunes in our Hymnal. Sir Joseph Barnby (1838–96), a great conductor and organist, was the narrowly defeated rival of Sir Arthur Sullivan for musical honors at the Royal Academy of Music. He edited five hymnals and wrote two hundred and forty-six hymn tunes, popular in style and very sweet in melody. Sir John Stainer (1840–1901), the noted musical scholar, excelled mostly as an organist. His writings on music and his hymn tunes display sound learning and artistic taste. Sir Arthur Sullivan (1842–1900) is best known to the world through his light operas, on which he collaborated with the celebrated librettist, W. S. Gilbert. In his church music, embracing a cantata, "The Light of the World," and many hymn tunes, he affects a pleasing tunefulness, strengthening it throughout with good counterpoint. His martial tune to "Onward, Christian soldiers," is universally popular.

Contemporaneous with these five leaders were many other composers, who wrought in much the same general style. The "Gloria Patri," by Henry W. Greatorex (1816–57), one of his five tunes in the Hymnal, is becoming as popular in Methodist worship as that by Charles Meineke. Of the three tunes of Sir George Job Elvey (1816–93), "Diademata" (179) and "St. George's Windsor" (636) are widely used. We have five hymn tunes and two chants from Edward John Hopkins (1818–1901), among them "Ellers" (38), "St. Athanasius" (77), and "St. Leonard" (472), all of them melodious in a most winsome way. From Richard Redhead we have only one tune, "Gethsemane" (280); though his tunes, always strong and usually interesting, are worthy of a larger place in Methodist music. His distinctive style is marked by plain simplicity of harmony, and often

by the effective repetition of the first phrase at the
end of the tune. Sir Henry W. Baker (1821–77) wrote
our plaintive melodies, "Stephanos" (293) and "Hes-

ORIGINAL FORM OF THE TUNE "EWING"

perus" (372), though they were harmonized by Monk. "Eventide" (50), as sung to "Abide with me," has become the most popular of our four tunes by William Henry Monk (1823–89). The tune originally written to "Abide with me" by the Rev. Henry Francis Lyte, author of the words, when near his death, has become almost forgotten. Monk's adaptation of Peter Ritter's (1760–1846) old German chorale "Hursley" (47) to the words "Sun of my soul" is known to every churchman.

Our one tune from Alexander Ewing (1830–95), named for its composer "Ewing" (612) and sung to "Jerusalem the golden," is of unusual strength both in melody and harmony. Originally it was written in three-two time, and therefore with an entirely different rhythm from the modern fashion of singing it. The changes to our present version were not sanctioned by the composer, even though they have been by hymnal editors and by popular usage. The composer said of the tune in its new form, "It now seems to me a good deal like a polka."[1] One needs but to sing the words in the first line of each verse to see how admirably the melody is in accord with the words, while the counterpoint of bass against soprano will be found to be excellent. A. L. Peace (1844–   ) has given us two melodies, one of them "Margaret" (481) sung to George Matheson's "O Love, that wilt not let me go" being less characteristically English than the other, "Green Hill" (314, etc). The popularity of the

---

[1] Cf. "Hymn Tunes and their Story," by James T. Lightwood. Published by Charles H. Kelly, London, 1905.

tune "Margaret" is probably due to its adaptability to these wonderful words, catching the spirit of yearning love in the rhythmic suspensions on the half notes.

Arthur H. Mann (1850–   ) wrote four of our tunes, the best known being "Angel's Story (350). All of these great exponents of the modern English hymn tune, that we have cited, were organists in English churches with the possible exception of Baker, who was a clergyman. "Bentley" (454), "Christ Church" (178), and "Nativity" (108) are among the other excellent tunes from this great English school not included in the work of the composers already mentioned.

Sir Frederick Bridge, since 1875 organist in Westminster Abbey, the musical editor of the Methodist Hymn Book, is represented in our Hymnal only by "Olney" (696), which he arranged from Gounod, though he has written many strong hymn tunes of his own. For his hymn book, and at his request, a truly wonderful musical setting of Charles Wesley's last, deathbed poem, "In age and feebleness extreme," was written by Sir Charles Hubert Hastings Parry, who is called by Grove "the most important figure in musical art since the days of Purcell." This has been wisely included in our own Hymnal, "Marylebone" (746). When the Tune Committee of the English Methodist Hymn Book referred this hymn to the musical editor, Sir Frederick Bridge said: "This is one of your treasures. Any church might be proud to possess a little hymn with such a history, and in itself so beautiful.

Let me ask my friend, Sir Hubert Parry, to compose a tune for it. It is just such a hymn as will appeal to his genius." Thus came to be written one of the most precious musical gems of our collection.

We have cited the German, French, Swiss, and British composers at some length. Other European nations have had a part in making our tunes, though it has not been sufficiently strong to give us a flavor of their respective schools. From Italy comes the "Italian Hymn" (2), by Felice de Giardini (1716–96), the widely traveled violinist, who died in Russia. "Vigil" (625) was taken from Giovanni Paisello (1741–1816), while "Manoah" (105) and "Linwood" (496) are attributed to the Italian operatic composer, Gioachino A. Rossini (1792–1868). Our former hymnals, both North and South, contained the tune "Sicilian Mariners," which to this day is sung by the gondoliers in Venice on Saint Mary's Day to the words, "O Sanctissima, O Purissima."

Russia has yielded "St. Petersburg" (134), by Dimitri Stepanovich Bortnianski (1752–1825), who reduced Russian church music to systematic order; and the inspiring national air, "Russian Hymn" (707), by Alexis Feodorovitch Lvov, or Lwoff (1799–1870). Bishop Daniel A. Goodsell has described to the writer the thrilling effect upon a throng of listeners on the shore at Portsmouth, as they heard this grand hymn played at night by the naval bands on board the Russian warships, which had just come to America during our Civil War to assert the sympathy of their nation with our republic, then in controversy with

European nations over the belligerency of the Confederate States.

"Austria" is the Austrian national hymn, written by Haydn, whom we have already classed among the German composers. It is probably the only melody intentionally composed for a national air that has been officially adopted. Ignaz Joseph Pleyel (1757–1831), who wrote "Pleyel's Hymn" (35), was also native of Austria, though like Haydn, whose pupil he was, he belongs to all Germany. Berthold Tours (1838–97), composer of "Rotterdam" (164), "Gouda" (447), and "Deventer" (708), was born in Holland, but after 1861 his career was centered in London.

Each one of the American composers contributing to our present collection, born in the eighteenth century, except Hastings and Mason, has given to our Hymnal only one hymn, each being fairly characteristic of the style of this period. They are as follows: "St. Thomas" (22), by Aaron Williams (1731–76), not excelled in this group: "Lenox" (294), by Lewis Edson (1748–1820); "Fillmore" (310), by Jeremiah Ingalls (1764–1828); "Coronation" (180), by Oliver Holden[1] (1765–1844), who also wrote the words of the hymn, "They who seek the throne of grace" (515); "Communion" (146), by Stephen Jenks (1772–1856), to which we sing "Alas! and did my Saviour bleed";

---

[1] Oliver Holden, a self-taught musician, was bred to the carpenter's trade. "The little pipe organ, on which tradition says he struck the first notes of the famous tune, is now in the historical rooms of the Old State House, Boston, placed there by its late owner, Mrs. Fanny Tyler, the old musician's granddaughter."—"The Story of the Hymns and Tunes," by Theron Brown and Hezekiah Butterworth.

"Woodland" (609), by Nathaniel *Duren* Gould
(1781–1864); "Armenia" (553), by Silvester Billings
Pond (1792–1871); "Duane Street" (306), the tune of
irresistible rhythm, by a former editor of the New
York Christian Advocate, the Rev. George Coles
(1792–1858); "Martyn" (463), by Simeon Butler
Marsh (1798–1875); "Holley" (74), by George Hews
(1800–85); and "Federal Street" (271), by Henry K.
Oliver (1800–85). The four tunes by Thomas Hastings (1784–1872) are "Zion" (91), "Ortonville" (135),
"Toplady" (279), and "Retreat" (495). The student
of hymn tune history would find it profitable to play
over each of these tunes, and observe their characteristics as a class.

The foremost name in the middle period of American hymn tunes is that of Lowell Mason (1792–1872),
who became famous as the advocate of the Pesta-
lozzian system, the founder of the Boston Academy
of Music, and the editor of a whole library of hymn
books that brought him a fortune. In these works he
adapted to hymn words many melodies from secular
sources, dressing them in dignified form for church
uses. Besides this he wrote several hundred hymn
tunes that have met with wide favor. Hubert P.
Main has said of Mason's melodies that their "simplicity, sincerity, and appropriateness to their use will
preserve them for a generation to come." In our
Methodist Hymnal twenty-nine of his tunes are used
to fifty of our hymns. There is hardly an American
hymnal of good musical rank but contains some of his
melodies. In England, however, many of the best

hymnals use scarcely any of his tunes.   Already in the present Methodist Hymnal the inevitable process of selection has decreased the number of Mason's hymns from sixty-eight in the Methodist Episcopal Hymnal and nearly a hundred in the Methodist Episcopal Church, South, Hymnal to only fifty (including duplicates) in the present Hymnal, and probably the next revision will show an even greater decrease.

Our seven tunes from George Kingsley (1811–84), "Newbold" (24), "Tappan" (99), "Boardman" (129), "Ferguson" (172), "Heber" (424), "Elizabethtown" (546), and "Frederick" (584), have enjoyed a great popularity, especially the last of these to the words, "I would not live alway." Of these the first three have been musically deserving of favor. "Rathbun" (143), by Ithamar Conkey (1815–67), has remarkably caught the spirit and accent of the words, "In the cross of Christ I glory."

Luther O. Emerson (1820–   ) wrote "Sessions" (342), known as the "tune with a slur," which is widely used through the South and West to the long-meter Doxology. He has graciously sent us an account of how the tune came to be written, a part of which we repeat to illustrate the devout methods of some composers:

"In the year 1847 I was living in the city of Salem, Massachusetts. One pleasant summer Sabbath day after returning from church, being alone in my house, I took up my hymn book, and on opening it my eyes fell upon the hymn beginning 'Sinner, O why so thoughtless grown?' My attention was at once fixed upon it. I read the whole hymn through several times, and the impression it made upon me grew stronger and stronger at each repetition. I had a longing to give expression in some way to my emotions. After a season of prayer, I went to the piano and at once played the tune just as it came to me. There was no hesitancy about it, no effort made. It was all done in a minute. I played it again and again, and felt at the time it had life-giving power, and would live."

An interesting phenomenon of American hymn tunes has been the gospel song of the nineteenth century. Lively in rhythm, simple in harmony to the point of the commonplace, the bass sometimes strumming through many measures upon one or two notes, while the melody does the same, or gallops across the sweet intervals of a sentimental melody—with these characteristics the tunes of the gospel songs have caught the popular fancy and become an important factor in the music of evangelism. The gospel song has had many exponents, the best of which have been levied upon for the Methodist Hymnal.

The eldest of these was William Batchelder Bradbury (1816–68), who wrote ten of our tunes. His "Sweet Hour of Prayer" (516), "He Leadeth Me" (489), "Even Me" (346), "Bradbury" (677), and "The Solid Rock" (330) are among the best of this type. His "Woodworth" (272), written more in the style of his predecessors, though endeared through long association with "Just as I am without one plea," must eventually give way to Barnby's richer tune "Dunstan," which is given precedence in the Hymnal. "Converse" (551), by Charles Crozat Converse (1834–), lawyer, philologist, musician, is sung to "What a friend we have in Jesus," and has most of the merits without the disadvantages of the gospel song.

Robert Lowry (1826–99), a Baptist clergyman who died in Plainfield, New Jersey, composed the music of "Something for Jesus" (349), "One More Day's Work for Jesus" (419), and "I Need Thee Every Hour"(506), to which last he wrote also the words of the chorus. William Howard Doane (1832–), a successful manufacturer, wrote "More love to thee" (317), "Pass me not" (329), "Every Day and Hour," (490), "Precious Name" (508), and "Rescue the Perishing" (697). Ira David Sankey (1840–1908), D. L. Moody's musical lieutenant, adapted "Tell It Out" (634). If the reader will examine the successive tunes of these gospel song composers, he can plot the curve of the modern American prayer-meeting tunes, as it proceeds from the more dignified rhythm of church music to the "catchy," lively jingle of the popular ballad. George Coles Stebbins (1846–), a coeditor with Sankey of the famous "Gospel Hymns," has given us good examples of both styles in his "Evening Prayer" (55) and "True-hearted, Whole-hearted" (420). John H. Stockton, William G. Tomer, and Mrs. Joseph F. Knapp have each given us one gospel song. Naturally, the editors, in admitting this style of music to the Hymnal, have chosen the best, and have avoided the almost innumerable collections of words and tunes, many of which ought never to be used in divine worship. While the admission of "gospel tunes" lowers the purely musical standards of the Hymnal, it makes the book more adaptable to the evangelist.

The last half of the nineteenth century has given us some hymn tunes from American composers that are used in the best hymnals, such as our tunes, "St. Louis" (121), by Lewis Henry Redner (1831–   ); "National Hymn" (704), by George W. Warren (1828–92), which was written for the Centennial in 1876; and "Festal Song" (413), by William Henry Walter (1825–93), all three of them prominent organists. "Cary" (620) was arranged by Eben Tourjée (1834–91), the father of musical conservatories in America, who was employed as a musical expert in preparing the 1878 Methodist Episcopal Hymnal. His daughter, Lizzie S. Tourjée (1858–   ), now Mrs. Estabrook, wrote the stately "Wellesley" (98), to which we sing, "There's a wideness in God's mercy."

The tunes written especially for the Methodist Hymnal are generally of a high musical order. One critic indiscriminately dooms them all to unpopularity. Time only can decide on this point. Many of them are already in frequent use. Whatever may be their fate, they are as a class musically well written, melodious in the soprano, and strongly constructed in harmony and counterpoint. Most of them follow English models.

More tunes were written by the musical editors than all the new tunes by other composers combined, Peter C. Lutkin contributing twenty and Karl P. Harrington twelve. Some of these tunes are mentioned in the next chapter. Mr. Lutkin wrote the Choral Blessing, "The Lord Bless You and Keep You" (748) with an elaborate contrapuntal sevenfold Amen, as a farewell to William Smedley, choirmaster at Saint James Protestant Episcopal Church, Chicago. It was sung, all kneeling, after the benediction without Mr. Smedley's prevoius knowledge. Both Lutkin's "Belleville" and Harrington's "Palm Sunday" were written on the railroad train.

Next to these in the number of new tunes comes Alfred G. Wathall, the composer of the recently popular comic opera, "The Sultan of Sulu," who was born in England in 1880 and is a graduate of Northwestern University. In writing for the Hymnal he has achieved a new record for speed; for all of his seven hymn tunes were written within an hour, and, furthermore, they were the first hymn tunes he had ever written. Individual tunes have been written within a short time. The tune to "Abide with me" was written by Monk in ten minutes, and Dr. Dykes's "Lux Benigna" for "Lead, kindly Light," came to him within a very few minutes while walking down the Strand in London in August, 1865. But Mr. Wathall holds the record.

"Puritan" (713) was written during a summer vacation in 1904 at South Manchester, Connecticut, by Henry M. Dunham (1853–   ), a prominent organist, organ composer, and distinguished teacher in the New England Conservatory. He was born in Brockton, Massachusetts, July 27, 1853.

Of his own tune, "Holmfirth" (611), the Rev. Dr.

Benjamin Gill writes: "The hymn had always been a great favorite of mine. Two years before I had lost the dear partner of my life, who had walked with me for thirty years and more. The tune was written at once, and sang itself out of a yearning heart." One of the members of the Hymnal Commission wrote about this tune in a letter: "It sounds like Ben, and all good, old, strong, true things—like old times, and like the hope of better new times. Nicht wahr?"

The tune "Shortle" (664) was written June 27, 1904, by Charles G. Goodrich, organist, composer and professor of modern languages at Marietta College. He was born in Waterbury, Connecticut, September 19, 1869, and graduated from Wesleyan Academy, '89, and Wesleyan University, '93. "Crimea" (124), originally set to the words, "My God, how endless is thy love," was composed in Martland in 1901 by Thoro Harris, an editor of sacred music, who was born in Washington, D. C., March 31, 1874. William H. Pontius (1860, Circleville, O.), composer of "Eighmey" (412) and "Holy Hill" (13), is director of the Department of Music, Minneapolis School of Music.

The "Sanctus No. 2" (741) was written for the choir of Saint James Methodist Episcopal Church, New York city, in 1894; and "Washington" (444) was composed at the Centenary Collegiate Institute, Hackettstown, New Jersey, in 1898, to the words "Abide with me," but was revised several years later and set to the different rhythm of "My Father knows my every need" for the Hymnal. But the commission dropped these words from the book, and the tune was finally set to "My hope, my all, my Saviour thou."

The Rev. Dr. Lorin Webster (Claremont, N. H., July 29, 1857–   ), who graduated from Saint Paul's School, Concord, '76, from Trinity College, '80, and from Berkeley Divinity School, '83, is rector of Holderness School (New Hampshire). His account of his composing of "Service" (414) and "Ruth" (492) is well worth quoting: "I can never think deeply about the meaning of a hymn without having a musical interpretation of it come to my mind and soul expressing my emotions from the sentiment of the words. And so these hymns soon aroused in my mind a conception of their meaning in both melody and harmony. Frequently, after the first draft of a hymn, I change the harmony to give a certain part a more pleasing progression or to conform the writing to the laws of harmony and musical form, and I did so in composing these."

Of the other composers writing especially for the Hymnal a few should be observed. Dr. Maro L. Bartlett (Brownhelm, O., October 25, 1847–   ), teacher, musical conductor, and author of several books on music, is the director of the Des Moines (Iowa) Musical College. Mrs. Emma Louise Ashford, née Hindle (Delaware, 1850–   ), is the wife of Professor Ashford, who for over a score of years has been on the faculty of Vanderbilt University (Nashville, Tenn.). As an organist, composer of eight sacred and two secular cantatas, fifty songs and forty piano pieces, and an editor of three musical periodicals, she has become known to a large circle of church musicians. John W. Baume (Halifax, England, December 15, 1862–   ), from a stanch English Wesleyan family, nephew of the late Rev. Dr. James Baume, of the Rock River Conference, is now a Chicago music publisher, composer, and violinist. His most popular song, "If I But Knew," reached a sale of two hundred thousand copies. Dr. Moses S. Cross, composer of the tunes "Resignation" and "Waratah," was one of three clergymen, sons of Rev. Aaron Cross of the Rock River Conference. He died April 20, 1911. John Spencer Camp (1858–   ), writer of "Abiding Grace" and "Sylvester," is a prominent organist and composer in Hartford, Conn. (see p. 202).

Rounding out the story of the tunes, let us consider their relation to larger musical works. Many of our tunes have been derived from oratorios, operas, masses, and other large forms; while, on the other hand, many of the hymn tunes have been taken as themes for development into larger works, or have been inserted with dramatic effect in the heart of some sacred cantata or oratorio.

The following hymn tunes, grouped according to composers, have been derived from the music set opposite their numbers and titles:

GEORGE FREDERICK HÄNDEL (1685–1759).

"Antioch" (107),	A medley from the oratorio "Messiah": (*a*) Chorus, "Lift up your heads"; (*b*) Introduction to tenor aria, "Comfort ye."
"Christmas" (115),	"Non vi piacque," from the opera "Ciroë" (Cyrus).

"Thatcher" (182),	From the opera "Sosarme."
"Samson" (298),	Chorus, "Then 'round about thy starry throne," oratorio "Samson."
"Bradford" (370),	Contralto solo, "I know that my Redeemer liveth," oratorio "Messiah."
"Dirge" (586),	From oratorio "Saul."

LUDWIG VON BEETHOVEN (1770–1827).

"Hayes" (131),	Andante movement in Sonata Opus 14, No. 2.
"Hymn of Joy" (160),	From the Ninth Symphony.
"Alsace" (518),	From the Second Symphony.

FELIX JACOB LUDWIG MENDELSSOHN-BARTHOLDY (1809–47).

"Consolation" (43),	From No. 3, Book 2, "Songs without Words" for piano, Opus 30, called "Consolation."
"Mendelssohn" (111),	From the "Festgesang," written in 1840 to celebrate the discovery of the art of printing.
"Wilson" (116),	Tenor aria No. 4, "If with all your hearts" (Deut. 4. 29), oratorio "Elijah."
"Bartholdy" (379),	No. 6, Book 3 of "Songs without Words," Opus 38, called "Duet."
"Intercession New" (509),	Latter half from No. 19, recitative and chorus in oratorio "Elijah" to words, "Open the heavens and send us relief" (1 Chron. 4. 27).

LOUIS SPOHR (1784–1859).

"Simpson" (309),	From sacred cantata "Crucifixion."
"Spohr" (320),	Solo, "If all thy friends forsake thee," oratorio "Calvary."
"Waring" (465),	Slow movement of string quartette in A minor.

FRANCIS JOSEPH HAYDN (1732–1809).

"Creation" (84),   Chorus No. 14, Allegro "The
                                heavens are telling," ora-
                                torio "Creation."

CARL MARIA VON WEBER (1786–1826).

"Seymour" (267),   From the opera "Oberon."
"Jewett" (524),   Contralto aria, from the opera
                                "Der Freischütz."

ROBERT SCHUMANN (1810–56).

"Canonbury" (42),   "Nachtstück" (Night-piece),
                                Opus 23, No. 4 for piano.

CHARLES GOUNOD (1818–93).

"Olney" (696),   From song, "There is a green
                                hill far away."

SIR JOHN STAINER (1840–1901).

"Cross of Jesus" (98),   From choral hymn, "In the
                                cross of Christ I glory," in
                                sacred c a n t a t a "Cruci-
                                fixion."

IGNACE J. PLEYEL (1757–1831).

"Pleyel's Hymn" (35),   Slow movement of quartette,
                                Opus 7, No. 4.

LOUIS MOREAU GOTTSCHALK (1829–69).

"Mercy" (562),   Piano piece, "Last Hope."

JEAN JACQUES ROUSSEAU (1712–78).

"Greenville" (39),   Originally occurs with slight
                                differences in Scene 8 of
                                "Le Devin du Village," by
                                Rousseau, which was played
                                before King Louis of France
                                in Fontainebleau in 1752,
                                and for the last time after
                                six decades of popularity in
                                1828, when some wag cast a
                                huge powdered periwig on
                                the stage, thus fatally ridi-

culing the opera. Berlioz, accused of doing this, proved his innocence in his "Memoirs." The tune, in arrangement more like its present hymn-form, became popular in London in 1812 as a pianoforte piece, entitled "Rousseau's Dream."

GEORGE JAMES WEBB (1803–87).

"Webb" (386),   From a secular song, "'Tis dawn, the lark is singing," written during an ocean voyage.

ISAAC BAKER WOODBURY (1819–58).

"Siloam" (281),   Originally sung to G e o r g e Herbert's words, "Sweet day, so cool, so calm, so bright," written in storm at sea.

THOMAS A. ARNE (1710–78).

"Arlington" (354),   From Overture to Opera "Artaxerxes."

SAMUEL WEBBE (1740–1816).

"Melcombe" (95),   From Mass to words, "O salutaris hostia," 1791.

HANS LEO HASSLER (1564–1612).

"Passion Chorale" (151),   A love song, "Mein G'muth ist mir verwirret," from his "Lustgarten."

FREDERICK BURGMÜLLER (1804–24).

"Emmons" (532),   From one of his instrumental marches.

"Old Hundred" (16),   From popular French song: "Il n'y a icy celluy qui n'ai sa belle."

Some of our tunes, as "Mendebras" (68), were taken from German folk song. Of these Professor John Stuart Blackie, himself a hymn-writer, has said: "Many of these melodies, though used on convivial occasions, have a solemnity about them, in virtue of which they are well fitted for the service of the sanctuary."

The use of our hymn tunes as themes for elaboration or as dramatic interludes in larger works is a study, which, if detailed in full, would lure the student through innumerable oratorios, sacred cantatas, organ sonatas, orchestral symphonies, and other large works, and would necessitate the expansion of this chapter far beyond its due proportions, so extensively have composers made use of these attractive thematic sources.   We cite, however, a few examples:

"EIN' FESTE BURG" (101).   Attributed to Martin Luther (1483–1546).   Meyerbeer took this as the central musical theme of his opera "The Huguenots."   Mendelssohn used it in his "Reformation Symphony," and Wagner in his "Kaiser March," Bach in various ways in his sacred cantata to the same words, and Dudley Buck makes it the climax of a male quartette.

"AMERICA" (702), attributed to Henry Carey (1685–1743). Used by Beethoven for piano variations in C major, and by Weber in his "Jubel Overture."   Adolph Hesse (1809–63) ingeniously elaborated the theme into a brilliant concert piece for the organ.

"OLD HUNDRED" (16).   Forms the climax to Leopold Damrosch's setting of Bayard Taylor's "National Ode," written for the Centennial in 1876.

"St. Ann "(214). By William Croft (1678–1727). J. Sebastian Bach's "Fugue in E Flat major," written in the last period of his life, is known as the "St. Ann's Fugue," because of the use of this theme in the three movements (1) broad and stately, (2) graceful, (3) rhythmic and brilliant.

"Munich" (151). Known in Germany as the "Königsberg Chorale." In Mendelssohn's oratorio "Elijah," as Choral No. 15, it is sung to the words, "Cast thy burden upon the Lord." This arrangement is nearly the same as appears in our Hymnal, where it is attributed to him.

"Silent Night" (123). By Franz Gruber (1787–1863), often called "Holy Night." John Hyatt Brewer has written a Christmas cantata, "Holy Night," based upon this theme.

"Russian Hymn" (707). By Alexis F. Lwoff (1799–1870). Used in piano piece, "The Czarina," by Ganne and in several symphonic works.

"Crusader's Hymn" (118). Liszt has used the melody as a trio in the oratorio "Saint Elizabeth" to the "March of the Crusaders."

"Passion Chorale" (151). By Hans Leo Hassler (1564–1612). Used by Johann Sebastian Bach several times in his "Passion Music according to the Gospel of Saint Matthew": No. 21, "Acknowledge me, my Keeper"; No. 53, "Commit thy ways, O pilgrim"; No. 63, "O Head, all bruised and wounded"; No. 72, "When I, too, am departing." Each number is sung in a lower key than the preceding number.

"Decius" (93) or "St. Peter" (97). By Nicolaus Decius (16th century). In Mendelssohn's oratorio "Saint Paul," used as Chorale No. 3 to the words similar to our own hymn (93), "To God on high be thanks."

"Nun Danket" (30). By Johann Crüger (1598–1662). Used by Mendelssohn as Chorale No. 8 in his Opus 52, the "Lobgesang," or "Hymn of Praise," to the words, "Let all men praise the Lord," which is Alfred Novello's translation from the original of our hymn (30) by Martin Rinkart.

"BREMEN" (476). By Georg Neumark (1621–81). In Mendelssohn's oratorio "Saint Paul" this forms the Choral, No 9, at the death of Stephen to the words, "To thee, O Lord, I yield my spirit."

"MILLER" (17). Mendelssohn took this as the finale of his organ sonatas. It is said by one critic to have suggested to Mendelssohn his aria, "O rest in the Lord."

"PORTUGUESE HYMN" (125). Often called "Adeste Fideles." One of the Christmas melodies in Guilmant's organ offertory, "Christmas Hymns." John Spencer Camp uses it in his sacred cantata, "The Prince of Peace."

"CORONATION" (180). By Oliver Holden (1765–1844). John Spencer Camp introduces this also in his "Prince of Peace." He is the composer of our hymn tunes, "Abiding Grace" (504) and "Sylvester" (571), both written especially for the Methodist Hymnal.

CHAPTER IX

THE TITLES OF THE TUNES

Derived from the Hymns—Authors and Composers—
From Persons—Places—Hills—Rivers, Etc.—
Method in Choosing Names

In the new Methodist Hymnal the titles of the hymns are no longer used, as in previous Hymnals. But, as titles are still applied to the tunes, why should we not know more about these tune names, their use, and their meaning?

There is a great confusion in the naming of tunes, for in many instances the same name serves to designate several different tunes while, on the other hand, there are often many tunes bearing the same name. When the naming of psalm tunes was first introduced in Este's Psalter (1592), it would have been simple enough to avoid this; but now when literally thousands of hymn tunes are being published each year, confusion is inevitable. Nevertheless, it is undoubtedly increased by the carelessness of editors.

In the Methodist Hymnal the editors have taken great care in the choice of names. Only one name, "Stanley," has had to serve two tunes, although in the Wesleyan Methodist Hymn Book there are twenty names that must stand for two or more tunes, and in some other books there are even more. One tune appears in our Hymnal under two names, "St. Peter" and "Decius," although this is somewhat justified by the difference in musical arrangement. In choosing names for the new tunes the editors have made peculiarly fitting selections. One quarter, however, of the names chosen for new tunes in this Hymnal are already attached to other tunes in other books, as "Temple," "Racine," "Ruth," "Middletown," "Resignation," "Praise," "Worship," "Stella," "Nashville," "Plymouth," "Washington," and "Evanston," the last two having been applied to other tunes in the old Methodist Hymnals of both North and South.

Usually, the editors have followed good precedent in the choice of names for the old tunes also. "Cobern," however, is among the exceptions. Dr. Gauntlett's tune, so named in our Hymnal, has appeared in many other books, and, so far as we have observed, always under the name of "Houghton." It is so named in the Methodist Episcopal Hymnal of 1878, but is wrongly attributed there to William Gardiner, instead of Henry J. Gauntlett.

To illustrate the Babel of names that confuse the psalmodist, we have examined every tune title in twenty American hymnals, published within as many years. As a result, we find that, on the average, about fourteen tunes in each of these books are either tunes contained in the Methodist Hymnal but bearing different titles, or tunes not contained in our Hymnal but bearing the same titles as other tunes in the Hymnal. There are over twice as many of the former as of the latter.

Comparing the titles in our Hymnal with those in the Methodist Hymn Book of England, we find forty-six tunes common to both hymnals that bear different titles, three of these titles, however, being very similar; and we find forty-nine titles referring to entirely different tunes in the books in which they respectively appear.

In spite of this confusion, most of the best hymns retain their original names, and to many of these names there attaches some peculiar interest relating to the composer or to the hymn. As so few of the constant users of the Hymnal have given thought to the meaning of the tune names, a glance at this field may not prove unprofitable.

Just a little more than one quarter of our tunes have clearly derived their titles from one of the hymns to which they are set in our Hymnal. Where a tune is used for more than one hymn, naturally such a title can be appropriate to only one of these hymns. Thirty-one of these titles make use of the English words of the first line, either entire or in part, as "Blessed Assurance," "Holy Spirit, Faithful Guide" or "Sweet Hour of Prayer"; and ten of them use the words of the refrain for a title, as "Close to Thee," or "Loving Kindness." These follow the German method of naming the chorales from the first lines of the hymn. Thus we have in our alphabetical list of tune titles, "Nun Danket" (Now thank we), "Ein' Feste Burg" (A mighty fortress), etc. All five of the German titles in our Hymnal are appropriate to the words. Of other titles suggested by the hymns fourteen refer to some act of worship, as "Praise" or "Baptism"; ten to some Christian virtue, as "Fortitude" or "Implicit Trust", nine to heaven, as "Paradise" or "Homeland"; and ten to the time of day, as "Morning Hymn" or "Nightfall." The Wesleyan Methodist Hymn Book, curiously enough, contains a tune by Mr. West, entitled "Sunset" to words that describe the sunrise.

The relation of some of the titles to the words is less obvious. "Old Hundred" or "Old Hundredth" is the tune to the hundredth psalm, of which Hymn No. 16 is a metrical version. "Joshua" is indicated, though not mentioned, in the hymn poem of John Hay set to a tune of that name. "Patmos" is suggested by the vision in the words, "I saw the holy city." "Palm Sunday" is meant in the words: "There was a time when children sang."

Many of our tune names, that have been derived from their original hymns, illustrate the chief disadvantage of this method of naming, in that the tunes have been set to wholly different hymns in our Hymnal, to which their titles bear no relation whatever. The following titles are explained only by the hymns, to which they are set in other books, but not in ours: "Angels' Story," formerly set to Mrs. Miller's "I love to hear the story, Which angel voices tell"; "Holy Trinity," to Charles Wesley's hymn to the Trinity, "A thousand oracles divine" (sung to "Azmon" in our Hymnal); "Radiant Morn," to Dr. Thring's "The Radiant morn hath passed away"; "Gethsemane," to J. Montgomery's "Go to dark Gethsemane"; "Day of Rest," to J. W. Elliott's "O day of rest and gladness" (sung to "Mendebras" in our Hymnal); "Blessed Home," to H. W. Baker's

"There is a blessed home"; "Nearer Home," to J. Montgomery's " Forever with the Lord " (sung to "Vigil" in our Hymnal); "Mercy," to Charles Wesley's "Depth of Mercy." Of the Latin titles two are taken from the words of the original hymns, to which the tunes are not set in our Hymnal: "Dulcetta" (diminutive from Latin word meaning "sweetness"), originally set to James Allen's "Sweet the moments, rich in blessing"; "Aurelia" (Latin for "Golden"), to "Jerusalem the golden." Five of these ten hymns are in the Methodist Hymnal; and in the Hutchins Protestant Episcopal Hymnal nearly all of them are set to the original tunes here enumerated.

The English composers especially delight in the use of Latin titles. Of Dykes's Latin titles we have eight, and two or three each from Barnby, Calkin, Smart, and Stainer. Of the thirty Latin titles twenty-one refer directly to the words in our Hymnal. For instance, "Nox Præcessit" (The night advances) to the hymn "My span of life will soon be done"; "Lux Eoi" (Light of the East), to No. 567, whose sixth line refers to the light; "Munus" (Gift), to "Day by day the manna falls"; "Vexillum" (Standard), to "Forward be our watchword"; "Vox Dilecti" (Voice of the Beloved One), to "I heard the voice of Jesus say." Thus also, "Diademata" (crowns), "Stella" (star), "Rex Regum" (King of Kings), "Stabat Mater" (There stood the Mother), "Vesperi Lux" (Evening light), "Pax Tecum" (Peace be with thee), "Paschale Gaudium" (Paschal joy), "Visio Domini" (A vision of the Master), "Materna" (Mother), "Dominus Regit Me"

(The Master rules me), "Iræ" (Wrath), "Laudes Domini" (Praises to the Master), "Pastor Bonus" (The Good Shepherd), "Penitentia" (Penitence), "Vigilate" (Watch), "Lux Benigna" (kindly light).

Eighteen of the titles are taken from the names of the authors, to whose hymns the tunes so entitled are set, as "Gilder," "Copeland," "Toplady," "St. Andrew of Crete." Two of these, "Gerard" and "Godfrey," are the first names of Gerard T. Noel and Godfrey Thring, the others being the last names of the respective poets.

Thirty-three titles are taken from the names of the composers, two of them being middle names, "Sebastian" and "Baptiste," from Samuel Sebastian Wesley and John Baptiste Calkin respectively. Of Felix Mendelssohn-Bartholdy's melodies, one is called "Mendelssohn," another "Bartholdy," while a third is often called "Felix," though in our Hymnal it is known as "Consolation." This same tune "Consolation," and also "Cross of Jesus," "Samson," and "Creation," derive their titles from the original works in which their melodies first appeared, as we have described at the end of the last chapter.

Many other of the tunes were named for certain people. "Vincent" was named for Bishop John H. Vincent, for whom it was composed. "Sutherland" bears the name of Alexander Sutherland, D.D., of Toronto, secretary of the Canadian Methodist Board of Missions. "Evelyn" was named for a personal friend of Mrs. Ashford, the composer. Of Professor Lutkin's tunes, "Gleason" was chosen in memory of the late Frederick Grant Gleason, a prominent Chicago musician; "Caryl" in memory of a little child that died at the age of four; "St. Barbara" in memory of the Methodist saint, Barbara Heck, after whom is named "Heck Hall" of Northwestern University, where an important meeting on this present Hymnal was held. "Olivarius" is the maiden name of the composer's mother. "Patten" is so named for Dr. Amos W. Patten, chaplain of Northwestern University, and compiler, with Professors Stuart and Lutkin, of the "Northwestern University Chapel Service Book." "Camp" was named for a friend of the composer.

The naming of the tune "Theodore" has an interesting history. When the composer first played it over to one of the editors, the latter exclaimed, "That tune sounds strenuous!" This adjective, so often applied to President Theodore Roosevelt, at once suggested "Roosevelt" as a name for the tune. But as that seemed too obvious, they chose instead the President's first name, "Theodore." After the Hymnal appeared, the Rev. Dr. Benjamin Copeland, author of "Our fathers' God, to thee we raise," to which the tune "Theodore" is set, wrote to ask why the tune was called by that name. Did the composer know that the author had lost a little boy whose name was Theodore? The reply came to Dr. Copeland that the tune had been named for the President. Whereupon Dr. Copeland replied that the coincidence was even more remarkable because when Roosevelt was police commissioner in New York he had been such an admirer of the commissioner's integrity and devotion to duty that he had named his son after him. Thus the tune of the composer and the son of the author of Number 713 in our Hymnal both came to bear the name "Theodore."

The names of four of the makers of our Hymnal are to be found in the Index of Tunes, though I have been assured by other members of the Committee on Tunes that their names were not chosen while these four were present. "Upham" was given to one tune in honor of the Rev. Dr. Samuel F. Upham, chairman of the first Methodist Episcopal Commission, and a member of the later Joint Commission on the Hymnal until his death. "Parker" and "Moore" and "Cobern" were chosen respectively for Dr. F. S. Parker and Dr. John M. Moore, of the Methodist Episcopal Church, South, and Dr. C. M. Cobern of the Methodist Episcopal Church, all members of the Joint Commission.

"Fisk" bears the name of the Rev. Dr. Willbur Fisk, first president of Wesleyan University. The tune was first composed by Professor Calvin S. Harrington to the words "Teach me, O my gracious Lord," written by President Fisk's widow especially for the theological students of the Methodist General Biblical Institute at Concord, New Hampshire. The words were not acceptable to the Commission on the Hymnal of 1878; but the Committee on Tunes urged that the tune be included in the book. Professor Harrington consented only on condition that it be published anonymously. Therefore a star in the old Hymnal is all that is to be found in the upper right-hand corner of the tune "Fisk," where now stands the honored name of this sainted singer.

The tune "Shortle" was named for Dr. Henry Shortle, late of Provincetown, Massachusetts, the father-in-law of the composer, Charles G. Goodrich. Dr. Shortle as Sunday school superintendent, class leader, and one of the founders of the Yarmouth Camp Meeting, became known to Methodists throughout eastern Massachusetts. Many remember with emotion his power in prayer and testimony. He died in September, 1892, at the age of nearly 58.

"Emilie," written in 1880 by John W. Baume, in Fresno, California, where he was organist in the Presbyterian church, was named for the composer's sister Emily. "Eighmey" was named for C. H. Eighmey, of Dubuque, Iowa, who is a leading figure in the Methodist Church not only in his own town, but also in the State in which he lives. "Frederick" was a title chosen by its composer, George Kingsley, because it was dedicated to the Rev. Frederick T. Gray. The Rev. Samuel Rutherford, a much-persecuted Scotch nonconformist of the seventeenth century, wrote the hymn "The sands of time are sinking" which was long sung to the tune "Rutherford." In our Hymnal the tune is used to other words.

Forty-five of our tunes are named after saints, following a method of nomenclature especially popular with the English composers. This is less than half the number of saintly titles in either the Wesleyan Methodist Hymn Book or the Hutchins Hymnal. Here again Dykes is represented by eight, and Barnby and Sullivan by four each. Many of these saints are unfamiliar to most of us, and, indeed, some probably never received canonization outside of a hymn book. Some of our tune titles give only the name, and omit the word "Saint," which often precedes it in other hymnals. For instance, our tune "Jude," written by the English composer, William H. Jude, is usually called elsewhere "St. Jude," though the saintly title need not argue any relationship between the composer and the "three-named disciple." "St. Gertrude" (Onward, Christian soldiers!) was dedicated by Sir Arthur Sullivan to Mrs. Gertrude Clay Ker-Seymer, at whose home in Hanford he was a guest when it was written. Here he wrote also our tune "Hanford."

Many of these saints' names have been given to tunes from the names of the churches in which the composers at the time have been organists or musical directors. In "St. Oswald" Church, Durham, Dr. Dykes for years was vicar, and is now buried there. His son, a professor at the Royal College of Music, was named John St. Oswald Dykes. Sir George J. Elvey, succeeding H. Skeats, Jr., was organist from 1835 to 1882 at "St. George's, Windsor." William Croft was appointed organist at "St. Anne's" at Soho, when the new organ was erected in 1700.

Other titles have been taken from churches. "Asbury" was composed by the late Claude W. Harrington for a celebration in Asbury Methodist Episcopal Church, Rochester, New York. "Sardis" was one of the seven churches mentioned in the New Testament.

Nearly a hundred of the titles are the names of

towns or cities. Five of these are mentioned in the
Bible. "Nicæa" was a town in Asia Minor where the
Ecumenical Council of A. D. 325 established and
developed the doctrine of the Trinity. Hence our
hymn to the Trinity, "Holy, holy, holy," gives the tune
its name, "Nicæa." Most of the town names are in
Great Britain. England reciprocates, however; for
in the Primitive Methodist Hymnal we note that our
"Webb" is called "New York," our "Hamburg"
called "Boston," to which are also added a "St. Louis,"
two "Brooklyns," and even a "Paterson."

Some of the town-names denote the composer's
birthplace, as "Holmfirth," a town in the West Riding
of Yorkshire, where the Rev. Dr. Benjamin Gill was
born, and "Racine" near the birthplace of Professor
Lutkin. "Rotterdam" was the birthplace of Berthold Tours, the composer. His tunes "Gouda"
and "Deventer" also derive their titles from towns in
his native land of Holland. "Kolding," "Copen-
hagen," and "Kiel," all in Denmark, are the birthplaces respectively of Professor Lutkin's father,
mother, and the great-grandfather of Mrs. Lutkin. The
first of these tunes is sung to a hymn about the greatest of all birthplaces, Bethlehem. "Middletown,"
Connecticut, the seat of Wesleyan University, has
been for years the home of Professor C. T. Winchester,
composer of the melody of that name; and it is also
the home of Professor Karl P. Harrington, arranger of
the harmony.

"Prescott" and "Belleville" are towns in Canada,
with which the history of Mrs. Lutkin's family is con-

nected. "Orono," Maine, the seat of the University of Maine, was for years the home of Professor Karl P. Harrington. Barnby was organist from 1871 to 1886 at Saint Anne's, "Soho," where he instituted the great annual Bach Festival. The new tunes "Nashville," "Plymouth," and "Washington" commemorate in their titles the cities where the Joint Commission met in preparing the Hymnal, and "Evanston" a meeting place of the Committee on Tunes. It is unfortunate that other tunes of these same four names exist in other hymnals. "Hursley" was the place where John Keble, author of "The Christian Year," and "Sun of my soul," was vicar from 1835 until his death in 1866.

Of over a score of tunes named after countries or States, three are mentioned in the Bible: "Gilead," "Goshen," "Judea"; and nine others indicate the nationality of their composers. Also by titles taken from the names of cities, the composer's nationality is sometimes indicated. "Crimea" has no special significance save as it illustrates the fondness of the composer, Mr. Thoro Harris, for geographical nomenclatures, especially those of unusual flavor. Some of his titles in other hymnals are, "Takoma," "Sligo," "Berwyn," "Arizona," "Oklahoma," "Benning," "Anacostia," and "Quebec."

Half of the eight mountains or hills named in the tune titles are in the Bible. The river "Jordan," the brook "Kedron," and the pool of "Siloam" are scriptural waters. It had been more appropriate to the words if the titles "Bethel" and "Bethany" were interchanged. "Bethel," the place of Jacob's dream, is the name of the tune to "My faith looks up to thee, Thou Lamb of Calvary"; while "Bethany," which is situated on the slope of the Mount of Olives, is the name of the tune to "Nearer, my God, to thee," founded upon Jacob's dream.

It is interesting to observe the methods of tune-naming peculiar to certain composers. We have already noted the Anglican fondness for Latin and for saintly titles, and the geographical tastes of Mr. Harris. Richard Redhead was accustomed to use his own name and a number. Thus our "Gethsemane" was originally known as "Redhead No. 76," as it still appears in the Episcopal hymnals along with four other Redhead numbers. Lightwood in his book on tunes has called our attention to Dykes's fondness for naming tunes after places associated with incidents in his life. He says that Dykes's career may be traced in the names he gave to some of his tunes. Among these our "Hollingside" is notable as the name of Dykes's cottage, about a mile from Durham. Dykes once named a tune "Sekyd"—his own name spelled backward. The Rev. N. Curnock, he also tells us, chose for many of the tunes of the new Wesleyan Methodist Hymn Book names associated with the early history of Methodism, as "Castle Street," where stood for many years the Methodist Publishing House; "St. Antholin," the London church, where John Wesley preached so often; "Gwennap," the pit in Cornwall famous for the Wesley services; "Moorfields" and "Aldergate Street," where many of the greatest Methodist meetings were held in the earlier days.

The musical editors of the Methodist Hymnal have followed this precedent in the tune title, "City Road." Lightwood's notice of A. H. Mann's fondness for classical names is borne out by two titles in our index, "Silesius" and "Claudius." Thus from personal associations and tastes, or the ideas expressed in their hymns, has been wrought out for the tunes a series of titles that has puzzled many a devout Methodist as he has scanned the Index of Tunes.

CHAPTER X

DESCRIPTIVE MUSIC

A BATTLE has been raging of late years in the musical world over the question of the descriptive powers of music. The thickest of the fight has centered about "programme music." This usually consists in a symphonic treatment of some legend or poem, so closely describing in music its sequence of events as to enable the listener by means of a printed programme to follow the action described by the orchestra. One school scorns programme music as decadent. The function of music is to depict emotion; and the high office of pure music, they insist, is perverted by relating it to events rather than emotions. The other school, who for the time seem to be in the majority, ardently hail programme music as the music of the future, and some devotees bow down to Richard Strauss as its prophet. They would justify their position by citing the song, the oratorio, and the opera, wherein the music aims to depict the emotions expressed in the words; and they triumphantly quote Wagner's famous phrase concerning "the fertilization of modern music by poetry." Over these points the programmists and absolutists break lances. In spite of definite convictions as to how long programme music will maintain its vogue, we must be content merely to have mentioned this great controversy in introducing this subject.

In the hymn tune, of course, there is no such minute description of events or emotions possible: firstly, because the hymn tune is practically the smallest complete musical form; and, secondly, because the many verses of a hymn, that must be sung, each verse to the same music, often evoke entirely different emotions, so that a tune that would emotionally describe one verse might be entirely foreign to the other verses.

We have in the Methodist Hymnal, however, some good examples of the correspondence of the music to each verse of the hymn. Let us examine, for instance, the hymn "Fierce raged the tempest" (485). There is a striking contrast in the poetic emotion between the first half and the second half of each verse. It is the contrast between tempest and calm. The music has depicted this contrast. The whole of the first line of the music is in the minor mode, the rhythm is agitated, and in the upward tossing of the bass upon the ascending sixteenth notes in the first four measures one may feel the furious rolling of the waves. But in the second half the music entirely changes to correspond with the change in the words. The harmony is quickly resolved into the relative major key, bringing reassurance: the rhythm gradually calms down from three notes in the measures to two notes, and finally on the words, "Calm and still," to only one note in each measure, while the melody at last ends on the

"ST. AELRED"—John B. Dykes.

1. Fierce raged the tem-pest o'er the deep, Watch did Thine
anx - ious serv-ants keep, But thou wast wrapp'd in
guile - less sleep, Calm and still... A - men.

2 "Save, Lord, we perish," was their cry,
   "O save us in our agony!"
  Thy word above the storm rose high,
    "Peace, be still."

3 The wild winds hushed; the angry deep
  Sank, like a little child, to sleep;
  The sullen billows ceased to leap,
    At thy will.

4 So, when our life is clouded o'er,
  And storm-winds drift us from the shore,
  Say, lest we sink to rise no more,
    "Peace, be still."

              —*Godfrey Thring.*

third note of the scale, which ending usually denotes confidence.

Dr. John B. Dykes's melody "St. Andrew of Crete" (616) to the words, "Christian! dost thou see them?" represents a similar contrast, sustained throughout each verse. In three verses the first four lines offer some tempting question, which is answered in the strength of faith by the words of the last four lines. In the last verse the contrast is marked between the weariness of toil and the glorious reward for toil. These contrasts the music follows with great emotional power. The harmony of the first eight measures is in C minor; of the last eight in C major. The melody of the first part creeps along with hesitant steps of small intervals, never going higher than C, emphasizing the fifth note in the scale, and finally ending on the fifth, which as a final note depicts uncertainty. The melody of the second part, on the other hand, is militant, beginning with intervals of a fourth, a fifth, and a sixth; and it bounds forward triumphantly like a valiant Christian soldier about to smite the foe.

"Vox Dilecti" (304) to the words, "I heard the voice of Jesus say," is another example of a melody whose first eight measures are in minor, while the last eight are in major, thus illustrating a contrast in the words. Each verse presents in its first part the invitation of Jesus, reminding the human soul of weariness (first verse), thirst (second verse), and darkness (third verse). The acceptance comes in the second part of each verse, discovering rest (first verse), water (second

"ST. ANDREW OF CRETE."—John B. Dykes.

1. Christian! dost thou see them On the ho-ly ground,

How the pow'rs of dark-ness Rage thy steps a-round?

Christian! up and smite them, Counting gain but loss;

In the strength that com-eth By the ho-ly cross. A-men.

verse), and light (third verse). The cautious and the spirited rhythms, the plaintive and the joyful melodies contrasted in the two parts of this tune, bring the invitation and the acceptance into strong musical relief. Even within the second half, the climax which the music develops corresponds exactly with that of the words, both reaching their culmination in the third measure from the end on the words "resting place," "soul revived," and "life."

There is somewhat of a contrast, though not so marked, within some of the verses of Charles Wesley's "Jesus, Lover of my soul." In the first half of the first verse "waters roll" and "tempest high" are compared with "storm of life is past" in the second half; likewise in the second verse "helpless soul, alone" contrasts with "my trust, my help." Here, as in the preceding examples, the contrast is reproduced in the music of Joseph Barnby's tune "St. Fabian" (463) by setting the first half in G minor and the second half in G major.

Although the sequence of emotions within a verse cannot always be reflected in the music, for the reasons cited above, a good hymn tune should portray, or at least be consistent with, the dominant emotion of the hymn. Various elements conspire to produce this harmony between words and music. Let us consider first the use of the minor mode.

In the present Hymnal there are nineteen tunes using the minor. Eight of these begin in the minor and end in the major (Nos. 151—second tune, 304, 403, 464, 485, 616, 747). The other eleven begin and end also in the minor (Nos. 4, 152, 155, 254, 270, 273, 380,

476, 580, 595, 603). It is no accident that ten of these melodies of the minor mode are set to hymns under the following classifications: "Sufferings and Death of Christ," "Warnings and Invitations," "Repentance," "Brevity and Uncertainty of Life," "Death, and Judgment" ("Day of Wrath"), subjects that lend themselves most appropriately to the minor mode. Four of these we have already cited (Nos. 304, 464, 485, 616). Of the remaining five hymns the first lines suggest the reasons for setting them to tunes of the minor mode. They are: "O bitter shame and sorsow" (380); "Defend us, Lord, from every ill" (403); "Slowly, slowly darkening," the sunset of life (464); "Leave God to order all thy ways, . . . in the evil days" (476); and "The God of Abraham praise"(4). This last hymn tune, the naming of which we have referred to elsewhere, is a Hebrew melody, and is naturally in the minor mode, which predominates in Hebrew music.

Besides these melodies that are distinctly in the minor, there are several hymn tunes that contain so many chords based upon the minor triads that they partake somewhat of that plaintive effect so characteristic of the minor mode. Of this class we give but a few of the many examples: "Asleep in Jesus" (583), "Mourn for the thousands slain" (698), "O that I could repent" (265). The first line of each of these hymns proclaims its appropriateness to a tune with minor harmonies.

A tender, plaintive effect is produced by the use of a series of consecutive thirds in the upper parts; that is, the soprano and alto singing in parallel lines only two notes apart. This is made especially effective by ending the tune on the third note of the scale, as may be felt in hearing the following examples: "When I survey the wondrous cross" (141); "Jesus, thy blood and righteousness"—Sufferings and Death of Christ (148); "O that I could repent" (265); "One sweetly solemn thought" (620). To these may be added "By cool Siloam's shady rill" (678) as fitting to the tender suggestions of childhood for the reason just stated. There are also a number of hymns that successfully use the series of consecutive thirds to produce plaintive effects which end on the tonic, or first note in the scale, as, for instance, the communion hymn (239); "O Love divine, that stooped to share, Our sharpest pang" (457); "Unveil thy bosom, faithful tomb" (586); "Shall man, O God of light and life, Forever molder in the grave?" (596.)

The martial hymns, calling to arms, are usually set to music having a firm and even rhythm. The intervals are wider than in the intervals of prayer tunes, and the melody tends to follow the chord-lines, as we are reminded by the tunes set to "Go forward, Christian soldier" (387); "Soldiers of the cross, arise" (385); "Onward, Christian soldiers" (383); and "We march, we march to victory" (418). In the last two examples the bass, especially in the chorus, seems to imitate the tramping of soldiers. A peculiar device to represent a trumpet call is often used in music, and it appears in some of our martial hymn tunes. It may be described in technical terms of harmony as follows: While the soprano is descending three whole tones, some other part, as the alto or bass, also descends, making a major third with the first note of the soprano, a perfect fifth with the second, and a minor sixth with the third, and the same intervals with the same notes as they ascend to the original note, thus:

You may hear this trumpet call in these two examples taken respectively from the thirteenth and fourteenth measures of "Onward, Christian soldiers!" (383) between the soprano and bass to the words, "Forward into battle," and from the first six chords of "My soul be on thy guard" (493—first tune). We choose to believe that this device was not used in these places by chance.

A striking characteristic of the tunes of the morning hymns is that the melody tends to ascend.

Naturally, it cannot ascend on every step, but there is a distinct upward tendency that may be easily recognized in the following examples: "When morning gilds the skies" (32), "Hail to the Sabbath day" (66), "Welcome, delightful morn" (67—second tune), "O day of rest and gladness" (68), "Lord of the Sabbath, hear our vows" (73). If we regard Addison's "The spacious firmament on high" (84) as a hymn on the morning of creation, Haydn's melody may then be said to be an excellent example of the upward tendency of the morning hymn. All of this is not without its psychological reason; for as the sun ascends the sky, and as our bodies rise from rest and sleep, so our consciousness and emotional life in the morning feels the upward tendency of the beginning of the day.

For the converse reason the melodies of the evening hymns tend to descend. When the flowers are closing and the sunlight is fading, our consciousness descends toward quiet and repose. A reflection of this "shadow of turning" may be seen in the following examples, in which should be observed also two other characteristics of the evening hymn—a fuller use of the chord of the dominant seventh, and also a very narrow range for the melody. The plaintive effect of the dominant seventh is akin to the pensive sadness of the twilight hour. The upper notes of melody are less singable when mind and body are approaching a state of rest, when our lungs inhale less deeply, and our emotions are quieter. "Abide with me" (50), which illustrates all

of these points, does not in melody wander beyond
the interval of a fifth. Likewise the whole melody
of "Now the day is over" (59) is confined within the
interval of a fourth, and not more than five of the
twenty-four notes lie beyond E and F. "Slowly,
slowly darkening" (464—second tune) is also within
the range of a fourth, save for two low notes at the
end. "Peace, perfect peace" (528), a hymn for the
evening of life, contains twenty-one notes, and all
but seven of these are on G or A. This same difference in the range of the melody may be observed
between joyful and sad melodies, and between vigorous and quiet tunes.

The contrast between conjunct and disjunct
melody should represent a wider difference of emotional content in our hymn tunes than is sometimes
observed by composers and editors. Our Hymnal
contains many excellent examples of this distinction.
Disjunct melody follows, for the most part, the
chord-line, using intervals that are as wide as the
intervals of the chord, so that if several successive
notes of the melody are sounded simultaneously,
they form a good chord. Some of the best examples
are: "Dennis" (100), "Regent Square" (25), "Pleyel's
Hymn" (35 and 248), "Horton" (248), "Consecration" (348), "Geer" (376), "Gratitude" (410), "Mait-
land" (557), "Jewett" (524), "Warwick" (41),
"Nicæa" (78). The hymns to which these disjunct
melodies are set usually express sentiments of joy,
contentment, activity or exaltation of spirit. And
where these express ideas emotionally foreign to

such sentiments, there is usually not a complete correspondence between words and music.

Conjunct melody, on the other hand, follows to a greater degree the scale line, makes less frequent use of wide intervals, and uses passing notes more freely. Emotionally, it is better adapted to purposes in contrast to those of disjunct melody.

They who delight in the musical depiction of material objects or episodes may without too great an exercise of the imagination find some examples of the onomatopœia of music among our hymn tunes. Just as in poetry there are sometimes used onomatopoetic words, which upon being pronounced imitate the sound described by the word, as "hiss," "buzz," "crackle" (of a fire), etc., so there is sometimes an onomatopœia of music, that imitates or describes the words to which it is sung. How appropriate may be this device to the true purpose of music is a question akin to the problem of programme music. Its ardent defenders are quick to cite Beethoven's imitation of the lowing of a cow in one of his symphonies.

One critic, after playing Parry's great tune to "In age and feebleness extreme" (746), exclaimed, "You can see the old man halting on his staff."

The harmony of the first four measures of "Thou hidden Source of calm repose" (466) describes well the thought of the first line of the hymn. There is a suggestion of hiding in the harmony of the first four chords, as they fold over from the tonic to the unresolved chord on B flat; but the quick return to the tonic triad on F seals the impression of repose, because this is the one chord denoting rest, to which every restless chord must resolve. On the opposite page of the Hymnal, "Cast thy burden on the Lord" (468) is another example of the same effect of repose, wrought out in the first member of the first phrase. In the next hymn (469) some musicians may refuse to see waving woods and rolling oceans in the waving and rolling of the melody, or to admit that in hymn 112 (first tune) the next to the last measure imitates in the alto and tenor the rocking of a cradle, where the word cradle occurs in that line in three out of the four verses; but, nevertheless, the suggestion is there whether wittingly or not.

In "Saviour, again to thy dear name" (38) a contrast is made in the music between the thought of "We stand to bless thee" and "Then, lowly kneeling, wait thy word of peace." This last line of the first verse is echoed in the music, as the effect of waiting or expectancy is produced by ending the melody with four notes on the fifth (which ending is very rare). To the words "Not only when ascends the song, And soundeth sweet the word" (520) is sung a melody that begins on F, and steadily ascends throughout the first half of the tune to E, so that while the congregation is singing of the song that ascends, their own voices are actually ascending the scale. One needs to observe only the name of the tune, which is "Ascending Song," to be convinced that this device was intentional.

Let us not dwell too long, however, upon the

many possible examples of this "onomatopœia of music;" for these are elements that appeal to sensation rather than real musical emotion, and may be regarded merely as the curiosities of psalmody, or, when they are not purely accidental, as the tricks of musical composition.

The real importance in musical description is that composers and editors preserve the emotional correspondence between words and music and apply the great principles governing this relation. There should be no caprice in the use of conjunct and disjunct melody, in the selection of modes, rhythm, or tonal relations, or in the choice of harmonies with which the melody is clothed. Melody should aim not at external effect, but should seek to reach the inmost emotion of the soul.

From this it will be seen that in the work of joining music and words there is vastly more required of musical editorship than merely the ability to discover music of the same meter as the words, and to make this the basis of the union, else editorship is not worthy of the name. Many hymnals, however, have disregarded the most common laws of metrical accent in uniting words and music. To avoid these infelicities the Hymnal Commission has set some hymns to different music. Professor Stuart, in an article on the Hymnal, says that one of the reasons for adding the tune "Sawley" for the words "Jesus, the very thought of thee" was that in singing the words to the former tune, "Holy Cross," it was necessary to accent the second syllable of the name

"Jesus" in the first and the last verses. The new tune corrects this, while the old tune remains in the Hymnal as optional. There are still instances in which the tune is ill-suited to the accents in the poetry, sometimes unavoidably owing to the irregular accent of the poetry. For example, "Shawmut" (265) throughout the tune accents the first syllable of each line, to which it is sung. But in reading the hymn one would hardly accent "with" and "a," as the melody now compels us to do three times to each word.

Some critics of the new Hymnal have expressed surprise that a new tune besides the old "Antioch" should be added to the words, "Joy to the world." But they would wonder less if they would sing the "wonder" of the last line of the hymn to the old tune with this ludicrous effect:

"And won—and wonders of his love."

The new tune metrically fits the words, as the old tune does not. The new tune to the words, "Just as I am, without one plea," also fits the words, as the old does not, and besides possesses a dignity and real musical merit, which was conspicuously lacking in "Woodworth." The sacred name "Jesus" occurs as the first word in sixty-seven different verses in the Hymnal; but in nineteen of these the music makes it necessary to accent the second syllable, as well as in nine other places, where the name is sung. In one hymn (222) this occurs three times. Likewise "Father" is accented on the ultimate too many times. Sometimes the sense suffers from this mispronunciation, as in singing "Welcome, delightful morn," to the tune Lischer (67) one must exclaim, "Well, come!" as though the wished-for day had not yet arrived, and were still in the future tense of that other hymn, "Well, the delightful day will come" (540).

It is curious that the Preface of the 1878 Hymnal, and also of the present Hymnal, both refer to the union of words and music as a "marriage," and still more curious that both Prefaces speak also of the "divorce" of words and music. Some hymnal marriages truly seem to have been made in heaven. We cannot speak thus of all of our Methodist hymns, though many of them seem to have been inspired in the union of words and music. But of the Hymnal as a whole, and of the appropriate joining of melodies and poems, we may truly say that it is in violent contrast to the work of the haphazard matrimonial agencies that carelessly assemble certain communities of tunes and verses and boldly call them hymn books.

CHAPTER XI

THE FORMAL ELEMENTS OF THE MUSIC

THE KEYS—VOCAL RANGE—UNIT FORMS—REPETITION AND IMITATION—HARMONY

THE Methodist Hymnal affords the student of music an opportunity to observe practically all of the simple elements of melody, harmony, and form; and a critical analysis of the hymn tune, the smallest complete musical form, can be made very profitable as an elementary study.

In reading a piece of music the first thing to be observed is the signature, or the number of sharps and flats immediately following the clef sign, denoting the particular key in which the music is written. Although thirteen different keys are available in music, each one of our hymn tunes begins in one of ten keys, no more than four sharps or five flats being used as a signature; and each of our tunes ends in the same key in which it began, except a few tunes beginning in the minor mode, that end in the major.

The following table shows the number of tunes written in each key in the two great Methodist collections on both sides of the Atlantic:

METHODIST HYMNAL (AMERICA)

G	E♭	F	A♭	B♭	C	D	A	E	D♭
137	128	98	85	72	67	61	55	31	30

METHODIST HYMN BOOK (Great Britain)

E♭	G	F	D	E	A	C	B♭	A♭	D♭
213	156	134	121	94	84	83	71	69	9

From this it will be observed that the most popular keys in both collections, G, E♭, and F, are those of which the tonic and dominant lie within the range of the usual speaking voice. Among the remaining keys, the Americans seem to have a decided preference for flats.

Investigations in the field of musical æsthetics have led to the acceptance of the law that the several keys are respectively adapted to express certain emotions peculiar to their own nature. Emil Pauer declares that "the key in music is what color is in painting," a fact recognized by Plato and Aristotle. Thus, he finds that the key of C major best expresses innocence, resolve, manly, earnest, and deep religious feeling; F major reflects peace, joy, religious sentiment, or passing regret; G major reveals sincere faith, quiet love, calm meditation, simple grace, or brightness; D major proclaims majesty, grandeur, pomp; A major voices confidence, loving hope, simple cheerfulness; E major tells of joy, magnificence, splendor; A♭ major is full of sentiment, dreamy expression; E♭ major gives great variety from solemnity and courage to brilliance and dignity; B♭ major is the key of open frankness, clear brightness, quiet contemplation. For this theory in æsthetics psychology has never given a satisfactory reason. Certain experiments tend to disprove that this difference in the tone-color of the keys is produced by absolute pitch, while, on the other hand, the tempered scale should leave no differences between scales, save that of pitch. But the fact remains that in the various keys a difference of emotional adaptability exists, and is recognized by nearly all true musicians. The best composers observe this principle in their work. Our hymn tunes illustrate in many instances a psychological nicety in the choice of keys.

Some composers, however, have utterly disregarded the fitness of the keys to the emotional intent of their hymns, while some tunes, as they have run the gantlet of successive editors, have been frequently changed from their original keys. Every melody must be brought within the range of the average soprano; for when it soars too high it is unfitted for congregational singing. Frequently this change from the composer's original key mars the tone-color of the tune.

Several tunes in the old Hymnals, North and South, have been changed as to their key in the new Hymnal. Some tunes appear in the new Hymnal in two different keys, as, for instance, "Regent Square," sung to hymns 113 and 169 in the key of C, which is emotionally preferable, and to hymns 25 and 662 in the key of B♭, which is more comfortable for timid sopranos.

Between the Methodist Hymnal and the Methodist Hymn Book of England there is a difference in the choice of key for the same tune in about forty instances. In four fifths of these differences, the

English book has chosen the higher key, as in the case of Carey's "National Hymn" (our "America"), to which the Englishman chants his patriotism a full major third higher than the American, singing in the key of A instead of our F. Thus in the matter of keys, as in other elements of hymnology, the Wesleyan Church has followed, more closely than we, the advice of John Wesley, who urged that Methodist hymns be sung in a high key in order to reach the full vigor of expression.

As we have noted, however, the range of melody should not exceed the average compass of the ordinary soprano in the congregation. The octave from E to E in the treble clef is the limit of comfortable singing for the usual congregation; and melodies that keep well within this limit have at least the benefit of simple range to help them attain popularity. "The Star-Spangled Banner" might, indeed, be our national song, were it not for its uncomfortable range of an octave plus a fifth. Our tune "Ewing" for "Jerusalem the golden," with an octave plus a third, leaves many a singer stranded high and dry before the sixth line is sung, while the greatly inferior tune "Martyn" to "Jesus, Lover of my soul" can be easily sung by a small child. The compass of the three lower voices need not affect the choice of key; but, by skill in harmonizing, these parts should be confined to certain average limits, the alto within the octave from A to A, the tenor within E and E, and the bass within G and C.

Trained choirs can comfortably exceed these limits, but not congregations.

The Hymnal may be used as a profitable text-book in the study of the smaller forms of music. The form of nearly all of our hymn tunes is known as the *period form*. In its simplicity, a *period* consists of two *phrases* of four measures each, or eight measures in all. While the musical phrase in its regular form consists of four measures, it may be extended to five, six, or seven measures, or contracted to three, or in certain meters to two, the end of the phrase being denoted by a cadence (the resolution of the harmony into a common chord on the keynote).

Of these many phrase-forms there are abundant examples among our hymn tunes, and to determine to a nicety the nature of each phrase is a mental exercise profitable and interesting to the student who has mastered the principles of phrase-formation.[1]

The phrase, however, is not a complete musical form. The period, or one-part form, is the unit of complete form in music. When regular it consists of two phrases, such as we have described. Nearly all of our hymn tunes are in the period form, and, owing to the variations in its two component parts, the period form assumes a variety of lengths and shapes in our psalmody. There are some examples of two-part forms, especially among the English hymn tunes. Among these may be classed most of

<hr>

[1] Cf. "The Homophonic Forms of Musical Composition," Percy Goetschius.

the tunes with refrain, the second part being the refrain. A very few of the tunes are in three-part form, the third part being a repetition of the first part, as "The Good Fight" (418).

These three compass all the forms exemplified regularly in our Hymnal. Some of the tunes seem to bear evidence of the composer's lack of familiarity with the laws of form. Still others are difficult to analyze, as "Ein' Feste Burg."

As an æsthetic principle, repetition is regarded as pleasing in art. This is especially evident in music and architecture, although poetry and painting and the other arts also frequently illustrate this principle. Many of our hymn melodies make effective and pleasing use of repetition. Only a few of the tunes repeat exactly both melody and harmony of the first phrase, as "Ein' Feste Burg" (101), "Holy Spirit, faithful Guide" (193), and "Maidstone" (469), the last example repeating not only the first eight measures, but also the second four at the end. Repetition to be most effective must be not exact, but should be combined with variation. In larger forms of music this variation is wrought out in rhythm, in form, in orchestration, and a thousand possible embellishments; in the simple hymn tune by (1) difference at the end of the repeated phrase, or (2) in the harmony; or by imitation of the melody, (3) in contrary motion, or (4) in the sequence.

(1) In the hymns Nos. 8, 36, 60, 127, 194, 195, 615, and 689 may be found a repetition in the melody of most of the phrase, but a difference at the

end of the repeated phrase, and often in the few
notes preceding and preparing the cadence. Sometimes in a repeated melody the variation extends
farther back than this, as in Nos. 27, 53, 66, 78, 431,
621, 640, 675.

(2) A repetition in the melody *with a change in
the harmony* is becoming more and more the custom
to-day, especially in the English tunes. Many composers of the older school would have made no harmonic change in repeating the melody; and even in
the contemporary tunes this has been consistently
avoided by some composers, as, for example, Richard
Redhead. Nevertheless, it adds to the richness of
the music, and is æsthetically good usage. In illustration of this, note the beautiful effect which the
composer has produced by clothing the melody of a
phrase in different harmony, when repeated in the following hymns: Nos. 30, 84 (second half), 97, and also
where only a part of the phrase is repeated, as in
Nos. 15, 77, 109, 199, 324, 406, 463 (first), 545
(first).

(3) Imitation is sometimes made by inverting the
melody. While there are no examples in the Hymnal
of a whole phrase being repeated in contrary motion,
parts of the melody are often repeated in inverted
form. The "Italian Hymn" (2) is planned throughout upon this principle. The thirteenth measure is
but an imitation of the first and seventh upside down;
the tenth and twelfth a repetition of the fourth; the
fifteenth a repetition of the ninth and the eleventh,
to each of which measures, together with the first

note of the following measure, the second and third are similarly related. Thus, ten out of the twelve active measures of this melody are involved in the principle of repetition.

(4) The most interesting form of imitative repetition is that of sequence (literally "following"), wherein the melody is repeated not upon the same notes as before, but upon other notes that lie one or more tones higher or lower than the original phrase or figure. In many hymns the melody of the very first figure is repeated in sequence, as in Nos. 161, 522, 566, 591, 603, 704. In others, not only the first figure, but also other figures, are thus repeated: Nos. 10, 62, 118, 298, 574, 578, 709. In still others the figure to be repeated in sequence begins the second half of the tune: Nos. 48, 130, 382, 387, 456, 518, 525. Sometimes the figure is so small as to lie within the compass of one measure, and is repeated in sequence several times in other measures: Nos. 63 (measures 8, 9, 10, 12, 13, and also in the tenor part), 157, 192 (measures 2, 3, 8, 9, 10, 11), 224 (measures 8, 9, 10, 11), 362 (measures 7, 8, 9), 452 (measures 9, 10, 11), 515 (measures 9, 10, 11).[1]

The tune "America" (702) illustrates both sequence and inverted imitations. Hymn tunes Nos. 57, 68, 640, and many others, illustrate both repetition and sequence. In fact, such frequent use is made of repetitions in various forms that there is scarcely a tune in the Hymnal that does not employ them to

[1] (The number of the measures is computed from the beginning of the first full measure.)

bind the unity of the melody, and to satisfy the æsthetic demand for repetition in art.

The harmony of the hymn tunes is richer and more varied than in previous Methodist collections, and the enrichment proceeds chiefly from the English contributions to our psalmody. It may be said also that the harmony of the new book is more logical and, for the most part, more correct. Such banalities in harmony as consecutive perfect fifths or octaves, augmented seconds, ascending sevenths or descending thirds in the chord of the dominant seventh, misspelling of chords—these demand editorial alertness to recognize and correct. Sometimes a composer is justified in making an exception to some rule of harmony, where there is good reason. Barnby, anxious to establish some ascending or descending line of melody in one of the three lower parts, or to follow some sequence, will often resolve a dominant seventh in unusual fashion. The first measures of "Love Divine" (355) and "Dunstan" (272) make beautiful use of the otherwise forbidden consecutive octaves between tenor and soprano. A few of the transgressions of these simple laws of harmony in the Hymnal seem not to be justifiable.

We may not dwell upon the meaning and use of each chord; but let us note one or two niceties of harmonic treatment that will serve to illustrate the importance of the harmony and its best usage. The chord of the dominant seventh has become of increasing importance in church music, since it was

first thoroughly established in the works of Monte-
verde, in 1568.[1] It is the chord of longing, of aspiration, and demands speedy resolution to the common
chord of satisfaction. It is less frequent in the slow,
dignified music of the Reformation than in modern
hymn tunes, wherein resolutions are made more
rapidly. When it is consistently avoided, however,
an effect of stately simplicity is heightened, just as
in Salisbury Cathedral, built throughout in the early
English style of architecture, the noblest beauty is
produced by strong, simple lines unembellished by
elaborations of the perpendicular style. "Marlow"
(8), "Winchester Old" (181), and "St. Anne" (214)
contain no dominant sevenths, while "Dundee" (96)
and "Old Hundred" (16) contain only one each,
and these were not originally so written. "Ewing"
(612), "Cobern" (92), and "Gilead" (202) have intentionally avoided the dominant seventh in several
places. Most of our tunes, however, abound in the
use of this rich chord, and, as was discussed in the
preceding chapter, to the emotional enrichment of
the music.

In none of the "Amens" in the body of the Hymnal
is the dominant seventh used. This is true because,
curiously enough, not one "Amen" is written to an
authentic cadence; for the plagal cadence is used in
each of the 557 different tunes. While of the two
forms the plagal cadence is by far the most
common in the "Amens" of other hymnals, it is

---

[1] Cf. "The Evolution of Church Music," by the Rev. F. J. Humphreys,
p. 76.

very rarely that a book entirely omits the authentic cadence.

All of the "Amens," with only fourteen exceptions, end on the same note as the last note of the tune. And each ends on the same chord as the last chord of the tune, except where the tune ends in the minor mode, in which our editors have every time added a major cadence for the "Amen."

The harmonies in our Hymnal are more close than one sometimes finds in the English Methodist Hymn Book. The tenor and bass rarely part company farther than an octave, nor the soprano and bass many notes over two octaves. There is still preserved, however, a freedom of motion in all four parts. As a rule, the bass should move in opposite direction from the soprano, whenever possible and consistent with good harmony. A bass that runs along on one note robs the harmony many times of the interest it should have. In the best writing the bass part has a melody of its own to sing. Owing to the peculiar intervals into which the bass is often forced, the bass part could hardly be adapted for the chief melody of a hymn tune, but not so the tenor part. The student of harmony would find it a profitable exercise to select the tenor parts of the following hymns for the melody of a new hymn tune: "Cross of Jesus" (98), "Bremen" (476), "Ein' Feste Burg" (101), "Nuremberg" (103), "St. Athanasius" (77), "Munich" (151); and in harmonizing this tenor melody they can be made to produce a beautiful new hymn tune. Such a harmonization of the tenor part of "Cross of Jesus" yields the follow-ing typical hymn tune:

PART IV

PRACTICAL USES OF THE HYMNAL

CHAPTER XII

HOW TO USE THE HYMNAL

PREPARATION—FUNCTION OF HYMNS—OMITTING VERSES—
THE CHOIR—GOSPEL HYMNS—HYMN STUDY
CLASSES—PRACTICAL PLANS OUTLINED

THE most essential condition for success in the intelligent use of the Hymnal in worship is *preparation*. Formal worship cannot reach its highest effectiveness when a pastor habitually neglects to prepare his hymns. And the first step toward preparation should be a thorough general familiarity with the Hymnal. It is a Methodistic axiom that every pastor should know his Bible, his Hymnal, and his Discipline; and yet it is often taken for granted that the hasty search for six hymns on Saturday night is sufficient for a knowledge of the Hymnal. In more than one theological school it is urged that the students form the habit of spending at least one solid hour each week in the study of hymns and tunes, a habit to be profitably continued during active pastoral days. Only by earnest study can be gained a practical familiarity with the hymns, their theology, their meaning, their music, and their relative effectiveness in varied forms of worship. Later paragraphs in this chapter suggest some methods of study for the individual student, as well as for class study.

This educational preparation once thoroughly accomplished, the choosing of hymns for particular services becomes something of the art which it deserves to be. In the more highly liturgical churches supreme attention is applied, as a rule, to the congregational hymns, the anthems, and the chants, and their appropriateness to the central thought of the occasion. This is made the more imperative because of the rigid regularity of the Church calendar of the Christian Year. But even where there is greater freedom in the forms of worship, as in Methodism, worshipers have a right to expect that the guidance of their spiritual thought throughout the service has been prepared beforehand with great care, and especially in the matter of hymn-singing.

A spiritual unity can be produced throughout a service of worship by a careful and prayerful choice of hymns, each fitting the occasion and performing some definite function in the office of worship and instruction.

Where there is carelessness or rude spontaneity in the choice of hymns, the fatal fitness of the hymn to the situation is sometimes painfully ludicrous. At Ossining, New York, during one meeting when the church was very cold, and it was deemed wise to shorten the service to protect the shivering congregation, some one inadvertently started this hymn,

> My all is on the altar,
> I'm waiting for the fire.

A prominent member of the New Jersey Conference,

upon his return from his honeymoon, gave out from
his pulpit the hymn containing the verse:

> O that I could forever sit
> With Mary at the Master's feet!
>   Be this my happy choice, . . .
>   To hear the Bridegroom's voice.

His wife's name was Mary; and, of course, had he
read the hymn through before choosing it, he would
have spared himself the jests of his friends for years.
Many such instances could be multiplied, were it not
so unwise to load our hymns with these humorous
associations.

In contrast to all this, however, the very psychological principle of association that sometimes
awakens the sense of humor can be and should be
employed to intensify the spiritual thought and
feeling of every service. This does not mean that
each hymn should be an epitome of the sermon or
its central ideas (though at least one such hymn is
often very effective), but, rather, that a unity of
purpose and feeling should be sustained throughout
the service, and that each hymn should be chosen
to reënforce the dominant theme.

Each hymn in the order of worship has a different
psychological duty to perform. The function of the
first hymn is clearly to create a spiritual atmosphere
of reverence and a sense of Christian unity. Were
each worshiper prepared for the service of the sanctuary by private devotions at home, the spirit of
reverence would be more intense at the very beginning of the service. But this is rarely the case. The

congregation usually assemble from their homes, where, perhaps, the last thoughts were of more careful dress, or the Sunday dinner, or some other household care. In passing through the streets a hundred worldly thoughts throng upon the mind, each insisting upon being borne into the place of worship. In fact, the writer has actually seen in the church in Concord, Massachusetts, where Emerson used to preach, men and women bearing their Sunday newspapers and mail into the sanctuary, there to peruse them during the forepart of the service. The first opening hymn should be an antidote to the irrelevant, irreverent, worldly atmosphere that often enshrouds the spirit of the churchgoer. Worship should usually be the theme of this hymn. Furthermore, the social sense of Christian fellowship and unity in worship should be awakened by the first hymn. Such hymns as "All people that on earth do dwell" (16), "Come, ye that love the Lord" (22), "Now thank we all our God" (30), and "Ye servants of God, your Master proclaim" (11) tend to express and arouse this idea.

The second hymn should usually be in the nature of a preparation for the thought of the sermon. It should be intense rather than exciting, quiet rather than animating. In a peculiar sense it tills the ground, preparing it for the seed of the Word. If ministers could realize how greatly the attention of the congregation varies on successive Sabbaths as a result of the second hymn, it would be regarded as an integral part of the sermon itself.

However important may be the two preceding hymns, the great opportunity of the hour of worship is the closing hymn. By an appropriate hymn at the close the message of the preacher can often be burned deep into the hearts and memories of the people; by an inappropriate hymn some of the elements of the message may be dissipated or confused. The closing hymn crowns and completes that which has been uttered before, and therefore makes it a more permanent impression. This can sometimes be strengthened by a reference to the closing hymn, or a quotation of some word or phrase from the hymn toward the end of the sermon. While such a device can be overworked, when judiciously employed it can be made very effective.

These general principles for the selection of hymns may apply to both morning and evening hymns. A difference in general character between morning and evening hymns will be more marked in those churches which observe a greater difference in the nature of the two services. The morning service is generally recognized as better adapted to more profound thought both in sermon and hymn. The Sunday evening service is a problem in most churches, and it is being met by making the worship attractive in a hundred different legitimate ways. The vesper hour is sympathetic to the tender emotions, and songs of heaven and our gentle hymns of rest in the Lord often make more beautiful the evensong of worship. Hymn services, such as are suggested in the end of this book, are often used to make the programme of devotions more attractive, and, under wise and devout leadership, more helpful to many.

Not only the choice of hymns but also the choice of verses in any given hymn is important. One must needs exercise caution in omitting verses from hymns to be sung. Each hymn in the Hymnal was prepared for the purpose of being sung throughout. Therefore there is but one hymn in the body of our hymns with as many as nine verses, four with eight verses, and fifteen with seven verses; and most of these are short verses. In spite of this, in some churches it is the exception rather than the rule to hear a whole hymn sung through all its verses.

Perhaps this word of caution might sometimes be applied to Hymnal Commissions. Our hymn (4) "The God of Abraham praise" has been made out of three other hymns in the old Hymnal (originally one hymn, as written by Thomas Olivers). To accomplish this, verses have been omitted, but with strange effect. The last two lines of verse four runs thus:

> And trees of life forever grow,
> With mercy crowned.

The following verse begins:

> Before the great Three-One
> They all exulting stand,
> And tell the wonders he hath done
> Through all their land.

Poor Olivers would have been horrified to see such a hiatus, making the pronoun "they" refer to "trees," instead of "his own," "his saints in light," as would be clearly seen were the omitted verses in evidence.

The most deplorable instance of faulty omission in editing the Hymnal is to be found in "Glorious things of thee are spoken" (210), where the editors have repeated the first four lines at the end, instead of the four lines that Newton wrote, rounding out the real meaning of the hymn so beautifully:

> He who gives us daily manna,
> He who listens to our cry,
> Let him raise the glad hosanna
> Rising to this throne on high.

Greater pitfalls, however, are dug by the careless omission of verses printed in the Hymnal. Leaders of prayer meetings, and often of formal church services, are apt to announce a hymn, and as if there were danger of monotony in singing too much of the same hymn they add: "We'll sing the first, second, and last stanzas," or some such glib formula for skipping, regardless of the sense or nonsense thereby produced.

If the reader will sing "the first and last verses" of such hymns as Nos. 137, 143, 165, or several others with gaps in the logic, he will appreciate some of the thoughtless effect produced by omitting essential verses. The third verse of hymn 79 is this:

> But when we view thy strange design
> To save rebellious worms,
> Where vengeance and compassion join
> In their divinest forms;

And yet a "first-three-verses" leader is likely to leave his congregation impending in midair upon this uncompleted thought, unless he reads over the hymn, and discovers that the third verse is impossible without the fourth. A similar catastrophe would occur if hymn 115 were ended with the fifth verse, or 257 with the third. A pastor once gave out the first and last verses of "In the cross of Christ I glory," and upon singing it was amazed to find the last verse exactly like the first, much to the congregation's amusement.

In order to develop the thoughts of the awfulness, the tenderness, and the worshipfulness of God, all so essential to the success of H. Kirke White's hymn, "The Lord our God is clothed with might," what verse of the hymn could be omitted? or what verse would you omit from 113 without slighting angels, shepherds, sages, saints, or sinners? Not long ago at a missionary meeting we heard "From Greenland's icy mountains" ended with the second verse:

> In vain with lavish kindness
>   The gifts of God are strown;
> The heathen in his blindness
>   Bows down to wood and stone.

To those who were closely following the thought of the hymn the effect was most depressing. It was like ending a joyful symphony with a dirge movement. Hymn 183 yields the same pessimistic effect without the prayer of the last verse. The fourth verse of "A mighty fortress" cannot follow any other verse but the third, because "That word," beginning the fourth verse, refers to "One little word" of the third verse. Thus in the practical use of the Hymnal if a verse or two must be omitted, it should always be done with care. How much better it is to sing all the verses!

It is wise for the minister to confer occasionally with the choirmaster or organist in the choice of hymns, especially if the form r be not a musician; for in many churches and by many pastors our richest musical gems are entirely overlooked, because they are new or unfamiliar. After the hymns are selected many pastors find it profitable to meet with the choir in rehearsing the hymns, where the delicacy of that overdelicate organization permits of his presence (and the value of a choir that resents diplomatic direction by the pastor is highly questionable).

The ultimate object of frequent conference between pastor, choirmaster, and choir should be to raise constantly the spiritual efficiency of the hymn-singing and other music of worship. This process should aim to elevate the taste of the congregation and to familiarize them with a wealth of good hymns and tunes now unknown to them. This can be done, not all at once, but gradually, like most other educational methods that are worth while. Learning new tunes can be made very interesting or very dull. One must be temperate in this, but constantly progressive. In the matter of new tunes some churches actually display laziness; others, in their zeal for novelty, rarely repose in the restful strains of the good, old tunes. A happy medium between the two produces the best results. A new tune

should be chosen with care, and, once learned,
should be frequently repeated at different services
until fixed and familiar. It is the new tunes, and
not the new hymns, that pastors fear to choose;
and many a good hymn is not available because the
pastor is afraid to learn the tune. The musical
ignorance of some congregations to-day is as great
as the literary ignorance of some of Wesley's congregations, to whom the hymns must needs be
"lined out" in the ancient fashion. But that did
not deter Wesley from giving his congregations
spiritual truth in noble poetic form. And as for the
tunes he used, some of them were much more difficult than any that may be found in the present
Methodist Hymnal. None of our hymn tunes are
too difficult for the average congregation to learn
with the proper leadership and a little patience and
persistence.

One problem every minister is obliged to face, and
that is the use of the gospel hymns. In some churches
there is a constant temptation to use them almost
exclusively, "because everyone knows them." Gospel hymns are often effective in bringing men to
their senses, in driving home conviction, in pointing
the way to the cross; and many a man can testify
from his own experience to the helpfulness of the
gospel hymn. But for men who are growing in
mind and soul under the developing influence of
Christian experience they yield only a weak spiritual
pabulum. Their nourishing, enriching power is too
meager and unsatisfying for a steady diet.

Furthermore, the constant use of hymns, weak in thought and expression, tends to thoughtless singing, or the bad habit too prevalent among congregations of singing one thing while thinking of something else. The presence of a few select gospel hymns in the Hymnal may argue the adaptability of the book to prayer meeting services and Sunday schools, but does not indicate that these songs are best fitted for the Sabbath services of the sanctuary.

That the Hymnal is suitable for Sunday schools and prayer meetings has been demonstrated in several churches where it is so used both in the city and the country districts. Some churches regularly devote a part of every midweek service to the singing of new hymns, often prefaced by explanatory remarks by the leader of the meeting. This widens the hymnological range of the congregation, at the same time adding a novel interest to the meeting. The chief argument for the use of the Hymnal in the Sunday school is that it teaches the children to memorize the truly great hymns of the Church. This better prepares them for the higher services of the Church, and—what is of inestimable value—fixes in their memories the doctrinal teachings and essential truths of our religion, so that in most cases they cannot be forgotten. How many Christian men and women have been helped in sorrow, strengthened in times of doubt, or led to repentance and faith through remembering the lines of some hymn learned in the Sunday school! Contrast with this the prevailing custom of using through every Sunday of the year a group of weak, sentimental songs to be discarded as soon as the binding of the books wears out! Then one can understand the criticism of Dr. J. Williams Butcher,[1] Secretary of the British Wesleyan Sunday School Union, when he observed that one of the two striking weaknesses of the American Sabbath school lies in its weak hymns and poor tunes.

One time-honored custom among Methodists is falling into disuse—the reading of the hymn before singing. Even though it may have had its origin in the ancient method of "lining out" the hymn to congregations that had no hymnals, nevertheless it has had the effect of concentrating the thought of the singers upon the meaning of the words. Indeed, there are well-authenticated instances on record of conversions as a direct result of the eloquent reading of a hymn by a pastor before singing. The art of making this a helpful spiritual exercise is being neglected. And this may be partly due to our sense of hurry, the lack of time, the necessity of making the service comfortably brief. But in omitting this we are neglecting one of the most practical spiritual uses of the Hymnal. On this subject the biography of Calvin Sears Harrington, D.D., by his wife, contains the observation: "He wondered and grieved at the modern fashion of merely naming the hymn for the Sabbath service; he thought so much effect was produced by the careful reading of those words of

[1] Cf. Article "The Sunday School in America and Great Britain: A Contrast and an Impression," by the Rev. J. Williams Butcher, in the Sunday School Journal, New York, March, 1909.

doctrine, of worship, of praise, of holy devotion. It was to him a means of grace that he wished all to enjoy."

Many of the richest resources of the Methodist Hymnal are left untouched by the pastor who confines his use of the book to the six hymns in the formal services of the Sabbath. The human mind takes pleasure in classifications; and by employing groups of hymns bearing upon some given subject or related to each other in origin or form, a hundred bright, interesting, helpful services can be arranged for Sunday evenings or prayer meetings, that would familiarize the congregation with our hymnology and accustom them to singing hymns with greater attention to their meaning. A few of the many possible services with the Hymnal we suggest in subsequent pages in the hope that they may lead pastors and people to a freer use of the Hymnal.

A Hymn-Quoting Service

Some of the most successful midweek prayer meetings have taken as their theme, "My Favorite Hymn, and Why." Using the Methodist Hymnal in prayer meeting would be an innovation in some churches, but it is worth while for a service of this kind. After singing several of the old, old favorites, and after a season of prayer, the pastor may speak of the power of hymns over the souls of men to draw them nearer to the Saviour. Then, after more singing, the meeting can be profitably thrown open for any to speak upon the question proposed. Usually this is such a popular subject that the speakers must be limited to short testimonies. For hymns to be used in a service of this kind it is well to choose only the old favorites. William T. Stead, in his "Hymns that Have Helped," tells of a popular vote conducted by one of the religious journals of England, The Sunday at Home, on the hundred English hymns that are most esteemed. Those receiving the highest number of votes were: 1. Rock of Ages (3,215 votes). 2. Abide with me. 3. Jesus, Lover of my soul. 4. Just as I am (these three receiving about 3,000 votes each). The next highest were: 5. How sweet the name of Jesus sounds! 6. My God, my Father, while I stray. 7. Nearer, my God, to thee. 8. Sun of my soul. 9. I heard the voice of Jesus say. 10. Art thou weary, art thou languid?

Sometimes after a ringing testimony concerning some well-known hymn, it is well to start the singing of the hymn (with or without the instrument).

A HYMN-MEMORY CONTEST

In Sunday schools, or Epworth Leagues, or sometimes even in the church at large, it is helpful as a stimulus to memorizing the hymns to hold a hymn-memory contest. It should be announced at least a month before; better still, three months before if the interest can be sustained. A list of fifty hymns should be published on a bulletin, or printed slips of paper, from which as many hymns are to be learned as possible. When the contest is held judges may be appointed. Each hymn perfectly recited should count one hundred points, and for each word misquoted or omitted in the recital of a hymn five points should be deducted from the one hundred possible points for that hymn. No hymn in which more than five words are omitted or misquoted should be counted at all. Thus seventy-five points is the lowest count permissible for any one hymn. The total number of points of each contestant should be added, and the one having the highest score wins the contest.

Bishop Warren's little book, "Fifty-two Memory Hymns," would be an aid to each contestant and judge; and as only two of his memory hymns are not in the Methodist Hymnal, namely "O the hour when this material" and "There is an eye that never sleeps," his book contains exactly fifty hymns from the Methodist Hymnal. This should make the ideal list of fifty in a memory contest. Their numbers in the Methodist Hymnal are as follows: 198, 396, 407, 23, 415, 66, 646, 109, 637, 461, 137, 236, 446, 682, 186, 612, 375, 537, 533, 148, 107, 159, 373, 702, 535, 518, 449, 540, 68, 363, 350, 153, 188, 214, 189, 502, 385, 139, 348, 207, 233, 136, 99, 416, 98, 92, 636, 128, 141, 392.

Sermon Series Illustrated with Hymns

An almost unlimited number of sermon-series could be devised, illustrating doctrines as taught by the hymns, or using hymns as illustrations of the subject-matter.

Christ in Song

Rev. J. Lyon Caughey once successfully used a series of sermons on "The Characteristics of Christ Expressed in Song." On five successive Sunday nights his themes were: (1) The Best Friend, (2) The Living Lord, (3) The Perfect Saviour, (4) The Light of Life, (5) The Hope of the World. Each theme was elaborately illustrated by the singing of hymns from the Hymnal.

Church History

An interesting series of sermons might be preached on "Church History," illustrating it by hymns from different theological periods.

1. The Pre-Reformation Church.
   Greek Hymns: 616, 672.
   Latin Hymns: 166, 533, 612, 614, 599, 125, 483.
2. The Reformation.
   Hymns by Luther: 641 and 101.
   Later German Chorales (which are Lutheran in form and spirit, if not in date): 30, 476, 151, 93.
3. The Moravians and their Influence on Methodism.
   Count Zinzendorf and others: 148, 359, 221, 225, 435, 273, 252, 333, 345, 305.
4. The Wesleyan Revival.
   Charles Wesley: 463, 1, 466, 111, 511, 181, 262, 256, 355, 310, 301.
5. Modern Evangelism.
   272, 284, 329, 325, 334, 544, 548, 551, 383.

Evenings with the Great German Composers

Upon these occasions the choir and organist may render larger selections, vocal and instrumental, from the composer under discussion.

1. Ludwig von Beethoven (1770–1827).
   Use Hymns: 160, 518, 423, 204, 131, 88 (second tune), 40 (in the order named).
2. Francis Joseph Haydn (1732–1809).
   Johann C. W. Adameus Mozart (1756–91).
   Haydn's tunes: 106, 105, 84, 210.
   Mozart's tunes: 80, 458, 378.
3. Felix J. L. Mendelssohn-Bartholdy (1809–47).
   Use Hymns: 43, 116, 379, 151, 273, 111.
4. Georg Frederic Händel (1685–1759).
   Use Hymns: 298, 182, 586, 115, 370, 107 (second tune).

5. Carl Maria von Weber (1786–1826).
   Robert Alexre Schumann (1810–56).
   Weber's tunes: 524, 267, 545 (second tune).
   Schumann's melodies: 127, 435.

Evenings with the English Hymnists

1. Charles Wesley. Hymns: 1 (his conversion), 643 (his
   preaching), 463, 511, 181, 262, 355, 746 (his death—
   see pages 69 and 228).
2. John Wesley. Hymns: 45, 624—Translations, 148, 221,
   225, 305, 333, 345.
3. Isaac Watts. Hymns: 5, 71, 107, 141, 146, 393, 577, 604.
4. William Cowper. Hymns: 37, 96, 198, 211, 291, 454,
   492, 496.
5. Philip Doddridge. Hymns: 100, 108, 230, 233, 288, 312,
   396, 429.
6. John Newton. Hymns: 69, 92, 137, 210, 309, 507, 538, 574.
7. James Montgomery. Hymns: 97, 113, 188, 397, 431,
   448 (second tune), 497, 646.

A Musical Programme

For an entertainment, Epworth League meeting,
or prayer meeting, consisting of larger musical compositions from which hymn-tunes have been taken
(see pages 196, 197, 198, 199).

1. Piano Solo—Andante movement, Sonata, Opus 14, No.
   2—*Beethoven.* Hymn 131.
2. Tenor Solo—Recitative from Oratorio "Messiah," "Comfort ye"—*Händel.* Hymn 107.
3. Piano Solo—Song without Words, Book 2, No. 3,
   "Consolation"—*Mendelssohn.* Hymn 43.
4. Contralto Solo—Oratorio "Messiah," "I know that my
   Redeemer liveth"—*Händel.* Hymn 370.
5. Piano Solo—Song without Words, Book 3, No. 6,
   "Duet"—*Mendelssohn.* Hymn 379.
6. Tenor Solo—Oratorio "Elijah," "If with all your
   hearts"—*Mendelssohn.* Hymn 116.
7. Piano Solo—"Last Hope"—*Gottschalk.* Hymn 562.
8. Piano Solo—"Nachtstück," Opus 23, No. 4—
   Schumann. Hymn 42.

Sometimes the hymn is sung after each program number.

SPECIAL HYMNAL SERVICES WITH RESPONSIVE READINGS

The following services may be used in the regular Sunday evening worship of the church, in the prayer meetings, Epworth League devotional meetings, etc. Indeed, many of them have already been used by the author and others in such meetings. Under each number or subdivision a passage of Scripture is given. These may be read responsively by the leader and congregation, if Bibles have been liberally distributed; or they may be read by different individuals, to whom the leader has previously assigned these passages.

Under each subdivision a hymn has been mentioned that is peculiarly appropriate to the subject. Many have marveled that our Hymnal touches upon so many different themes. Some of these hymn-tunes are old, some are new. The pastor or leader should not hesitate to sing the new tunes, as these would broaden the melodic range of his congregation.

At the end of each service is added some topic for general discussion which may be used effectively in a prayer meeting. The best results can be secured if the leader assigns this subject beforehand to several people, who shall come prepared to speak upon it. In the case of the Old Testament or New Testament heroes it adds to the interest to assign a different character to each speaker, according to his own selection.

NOTE.—Some of these services with Responsive Readings, published separately by the Methodist Book Concern, may be secured upon application.

1. The Birth of Christ

1. Prophecy. Isa. 9. 2–7.
   Hymn 116, "Come, thou long-expected Jesus."

2. The Birth-Place. Luke 2. 1–7.
   Hymn 121, "O little town of Bethlehem."

3. The Night. Isa. 8. 22 and 9. 1–2.
   Hymn 123, "Silent night! Holy night!"

4. The Mother. Luke 1. 46–55 (The Magnificat).
   Hymn 112 (second tune, verses 1, 2), "There's a song in the air!"

5. The Shepherds. Luke 2. 8–12.
   Hymn 115 (verses 1, 4), "While shepherds watched their flocks."

6. The Angels. Luke 2. 13–19.
   Hymn 113, "Angels from the realms of glory."

7. The Gloria. Read the Gloria in Excelsis, Hymn No. 742.
   Hymn 120, "Long years ago o'er Bethlehem's hills."

8. The Wise Men. Matt. 2. 1–11.
   Hymn 114 (verses 1, 3, 4), "Brightest and best of the sons."

9. The Mission of Joy and Love. John 3. 13–21.
   Hymn 107, "Joy to the world! the Lord is come."

10. The Appeal to Our Hearts. John 15. 7–16.
    Hymn 122, "Thou didst leave thy throne and thy kingly crown."

Topic for Discussion: "What does Christmas Mean to You?"

2. The Life of Christ

Opening Hymn, 138, "Christ's life our code, his cross our creed."

1. His Birth. Luke 2. 8–20.
   Hymn 112 (second tune), "There's a song in the air!"

2. His Childhood. Luke 2. 40–52.
   Hymn 678 (5th and 6th verses), "O Thou, whose infant feet were found."

3. His Preaching. Luke 4. 15–22.
   Hymn 290, "How sweetly flowed the gospel's sound!"

4. His Miracles. Matt. 4. 23–25.
   Hymn 695, "When Jesus dwelt in mortal clay."

5. His Transfiguration. Matt. 17. 1–8.
   Hymn 129, "The chosen three on mountain height."

6. His Love for Little Children. Mark 10. 13–16.
   Hymn 230, "See Israel's gentle Shepherd stand."

7. Palm Sunday. Mark 11. 1–10.
   Hymn 150, "Ride on, ride on in majesty!"

8. The Last Supper. Mark 14. 12–26.
   Hymn 235, "Jesus spreads His banner o'er us."

9. His Passion. Mark 14. 32–42.
   Hymn 147, "'Tis midnight; and on Olive's brow."

10. The Cross. Mark 15. 22–39.
    Hymn 142, "Behold the Saviour of mankind."

11. His Resurrection. Mark 16. 1–14.
    Hymn 156, "Christ the Lord is risen to-day."

12. His Ascension. Acts 1. 1–11.
    Hymn 161, "Rise, glorious Conqueror, rise."

Closing Hymn, 180, "All hail the power of Jesus' name!"

Topic for Discussion: "Is the Historic Christ a Reality to You?"

3. THE PARABLES OF CHRIST

Opening Hymn, 290, "How sweetly flowed the gospel's sound!"

1. The Solid Rock. Matt. 7. 24–27.
   Hymn 330, "My hope is built on nothing less."

2. The Sower and His Seed. Matt. 13. 1–12.
   Hymn 221, "High on his everlasting throne."

3. Who is My Neighbor? Luke 10. 25–37.
   Hymn 690, "Who is thy neighbor?"

4. The Feast. Luke 14. 15–24.
   Hymn 256, "Come, sinners, to the gospel feast."

5. The Prodigal Son. Luke 15. 11–32.
   Hymn 255, "Return, O wanderer, return."

6. Lazarus, the Poor Man. Luke 16. 19–31.
   Hymn 628 (3d verse), "While here, a stranger far from home."

7. The Lost Sheep. Luke 15. 1–7.
   Hymn 300, "I was a wandering sheep."

8. The Wise and Foolish Virgins. Matt. 25. 1–13.
   Hymn 429, "Ye servants of the Lord" (1st two verses).

9. The Talents. Matt. 25. 14–30.
   Hymn 597, "Servant of God, well done!" (1st verse only).

Closing Hymn, 127 (1st and last verses), "How beauteous were the marks divine."

Topic for Discussion: "What is Your Favorite Parable?"

4. The Miracles of Christ

1. The Marriage Feast at Cana. John 2. 1–11.
   Hymn 667 (1st verse only), "Since Jesus freely did appear."

2. Healing the Sick. Matt. 8. 14–17.
   Hymn 54 (1st, 2d, and 6th verses), "At even ere the sun was set."

3. Stilling of the Tempest. Mark 4. 35–41.
   Hymn 485, "Fierce raged the tempest o'er the deep."

4. Healed by the Hem of His Garment. Mark 5. 24–34.
   Hymn 696 (3d and 4th verses), "And Christ was still the healing friend."

5. Feeding the Multitude. Matt. 14. 14–21.
   Hymn 325, "Break thou the bread of life."

6. Walking on the Sea. Matt. 14. 24–33.
   Hymn 61 (3d verse), "Thou, who in darkness walking didst appear."

7. The Raising of Lazarus. John 11. 32–45.
   Hymn 134 (1st and 5th verses), "When gathering clouds around I see."

8. The Miracle of the Resurrection. John 20. 1–9.
   Hymn 157, "The Lord is risen indeed."

9. The Ascension. Luke 24. 50–53.
   Hymn 170, "He is gone; a cloud of light."

10. Salvation—The Greatest Miracle. Luke 24. 39–43.
    Hymn 289, "Of Him who did salvation bring."

Closing Hymn, 512 (1st two verses), "To God in every want."

"In shouts, or silent awe, adore
His miracles of grace."

Topic for Discussion: "What is the Most Impressive Miracle?"

5. THE BEATITUDES

Opening Hymn, 502, "Prayer is appointed to convey
The blessings God designs to give."

Prayer.

Responsive Reading: Matt. 5. 1–12.

(After the responsive reading, let the congregation recite in unison each beatitude before singing the hymn; also the leader may make some introductory comments upon each beatitude in turn.)

1. Blessed are the poor in spirit: for theirs is the kingdom of heaven.
   Hymn 472, "I bow my forehead in the dust."
2. Blessed are they that mourn: for they shall be comforted.
   Hymn 526, "Come, ye disconsolate."
3. Blessed are the meek: for they shall inherit the earth.
   Hymn 685, "Jesus, meek and gentle."
4. Blessed are they which do hunger and thirst after righteousness: for they shall be filled.
   Hymn 233, "The King of heaven his table spreads."
5. Blessed are the merciful: for they shall obtain mercy.
   Hymn 378 (beginning with 3d verse), "That I thy mercy may proclaim."
6. Blessed are the pure in heart: for they shall see God.
   Hymn 360, "Blest are the pure in heart."
7. Blessed are the peacemakers: for they shall be called the children of God.
   Hymn 707, "God, the All-Terrible!"
8. Blessed are they which are persecuted for righteousness' sake: for theirs is the kingdom of heaven.
   Hymn 432 (beginning with 3d verse), "Who suffer with our Master here."
9. Blessed are ye, when men shall revile you, and persecute you, and shall say all manner of evil against you falsely for my sake. Rejoice, and be exceeding glad: for great is your reward in heaven: for so persecuted they the prophets which were before you.
   Hymn 415, "Faith of our fathers!"

Topic for Discussion: "Your Favorite Beatitude."

6. The Lord's Prayer

Opening Hymn, 497, "Prayer is the soul's sincere desire."

Prayer (followed by the Lord's Prayer in concert).

(This service may be used in the same way as the service on "The Beatitudes" with comments by the leader upon each phrase, or each topic may be assigned to a different person for three minutes.)

1. Our Father who art in heaven.
    Hymn 79 (4 verses), "Father, how wide thy glory shines!"

2. Hallowed be thy name.
    Hymn 180, "All hail the power of Jesus' name!"

3. Thy kingdom come.
    Hymn 208, "I love thy kingdom, Lord."

4. Thy will be done in earth, as it is in heaven.
    Hymn 524, "My Jesus, as thou wilt."

5. Give us this day our daily bread.
    Hymn 325, "Break thou the bread of life."

6. Forgive us our trespasses, as we forgive them that trespass against us.
    Hymn 98, "There's a wideness in God's mercy."

7. Lead us not into temptation.
    Hymn 431, "In the hour of trial."

8. Deliver us from evil.
    Hymn 577 (1st two verses), "O God, our help in ages past."

9. Thine is the kingdom.
    Hymn 527, "The kingdom that I seek is thine."

10. The power.
    Hymn 2, "Come, thou almighty King."

11. The glory.
    Hymn 49, "Glory to thee, my God."

Topic for Discussion: "The Power of Prayer."

7. THE NAME OF CHRIST

1. Revelation of His Name.   Gen. 32. 24–30.
   Hymn 511 (verses 1, 3, 6), "Come, O thou Traveler unknown."

2. Salvation through His Name.   Acts 4. 8–12.
   Hymn 1 (verses 3, 4), "Jesus! the name that charms our fears!"

3. Strength against Temptation.   Prov. 18. 10; Acts 3. 13–16.
   Hymn 363 (verses 4, 5), "O, utter but the name of God."

4. A Foundation for Character.   Col. 3. 14–17.
   Hymn 330 (verses 1, 3), "My hope is built on nothing less."

5. The Name Victorious.   2 Chron. 14. 7–12.
   Hymn 11 (verses 1, 2), "Ye servants of God."

6. The Supremacy of His Name.   Psa. 113. 1–5; Eph. 1. 21.
   Hymn 222 (verses 1, 2), "Jesus, the name high over all."

7. A Name to Trust.   Psa. 9. 7–10.
   Hymn 441 (verses 1, 2), "I'm not ashamed to own my Lord."

8. A Name to Love.   Psa. 72. 17–19.
   Hymn 137, "How sweet the name of Jesus sounds!"

9. A Precious Name.   1 Pet. 2. 1–7.
   Hymn 508, "Take the name of Jesus with you."

Prayer.

Closing Hymn, 354 (verses 1, 5), "O for a heart to praise my God."

Topic for Discussion: "Which Name Applied to Christ is Dearest to You?"

8. The Resurrection

1. Palm Sunday.   Matt. 21. 1–11.
   Hymn 150, "Ride on, ride on, in majesty."

2. Gethsemane.   Matt. 26. 36–46.
   Hymn 147, "'Tis midnight; and on Olives' brow."

3. The Crucifixion.   Mark 15. 24–39.
   Hymn 146, "Alas! and did my Saviour bleed?"

4. The Return from the Cross.   Matt. 27. 55–66.
   Hymn 152 (verses 1, 4), "O come and mourn with
   me awhile."

5. The Dawn of Easter Day.   John 20. 1–13.
   Hymn 166, "Welcome, happy morning!"

6. Christ Forsakes the Tomb.   John 20. 14–17.
   Hymn 165 (verses 3, 4, 5), "The rising God forsakes
   the tomb."

7. His Friends Learn of the Resurrection.   John 20. 18–29.
   Hymn 159, "Lift your glad voices."

8. The Significance of Easter.   1 Cor. 15. 12–22.
   Hymn 156, "Christ the Lord is risen to-day."

9. A Spiritual Release for Israel.   Acts 3. 18–26.
   Hymn 163, "Come, ye faithful, raise the strain."

10. Job's Faith in Immortality.   Job 19. 25–27.
    Hymn 168, "I know that my Redeemer lives."

11. The Coronation of Christ.   Rev. 5. 8–13.
    Hymn 169, "Look, ye saints, the sight is glorious."

Topic for Discussion: "The Comfort and Hope Begotten by
the Resurrection of Christ."

9. OLD TESTAMENT HEROES

1. **The** Saints of Old.   Heb. 11. 13–16.

  Hymn 187, "O for that flame of living fire!"

2. Abraham—the Friend of God.   Gen. 22. 15–18.

  Hymn 4, "The God of Abraham praise" (1st, 2d, and 6th verses).

3. The Faith of Job.   Job 2. 1–3.

  Hymn 370, "I know that my Redeemer lives."

4. The Victory of Jacob.   Gen. 32. 24–30.

  Hymn 511, "Come, O thou traveler unknown."

5. The Vision of Moses.   Deut. 34. 1–5.

  Hymn 604, "There is a land of pure delight."

6. **The** Obedience of Samuel.   1 Sam. 3. 1–19.

  Hymn 674, "Hushed was the evening hymn."

7. The Harp of David.   1 Sam. 16. 19–23.

  Hymn 71, "Sweet is the work, my God, my King" (2 verses).

8. The Twenty-third Psalm.   Psa. 23 (in concert).

  Hymn 136, "The King of love my Shepherd is."

Closing Hymn, 12, "O Thou to whom, in ancient time,
        The lyre of Hebrew bards was strung."

Topic for Discussion: "Your Favorite Old Testament Hero."

10. New Testament Heroes

Opening Hymn, Thanks for the Saints.

> Hymn 14 (second tune, verses 1, 2, 3, 5), "To thee, Eternal Soul."

> *The Apostles.*
>> Peter, James, and John. Matt. 17. 1–8.
>> Hymn 129, "The chosen three on mountain height."
>> A Tempest on the Sea. Mark 4. 36–41.
>> Hymn 485, "Fierce raged the tempest."
>> The Last Supper. Matt. 26. 19–30.
>> Hymn 233, "The King of heaven his table spreads."
>> The Disciples at Emmaus. Luke 24. 13–21 and 28–32.
>> Hymn 50, "Abide with me!"

> *John, the Disciple, Whom Jesus Loved.* John 13. 23–26.
>> Hymn 368 (verses 1, 2, 5), "O Love divine, how sweet thou art!"

> *Peter, the Apostle.*
>> Penitence. Luke 22. 54–62.
>> Hymn 491, "Jesus, let thy pitying eye."
>> In Prison. Acts 5. 17–23.
>> Hymn 310 (verses 4, 5), "Long my imprisoned spirit lay."

> *Stephen, the Martyr.* Acts 7. 54–60.
>> Hymn 416, "The Son of God goes forth to war."

> *Paul, the Saint.*
>> His Inspiration. Phil. 4. 10–20.
>> Hymn 187 (verses 1, 2), "O for that flame of living fire!"
>> His Preparation. Eph. 6. 10–17.
>> Hymn 397, "Behold! the Christian warrior stand."
>> His Victory. 1 Tim. 6. 11–16.
>> Hymn 391 (verses 1, 4), "I the good fight have fought."

Closing Hymn, 430, "For all the Saints."

Topic for Discussion: "Your Favorite New Testament Hero."

11. THE JOURNEY OF ISRAEL

1. **The Escape from Egypt.**   Exod. 14. 22–30.
   Hymn 163 (verse 1), "Come, ye faithful, raise the strain."

2. **Heavenly Manna.**   Exod. 16. 11–18.
   Hymn 438 (verses 1, 2), "Day by day the manna fell."

3. **In the Wilderness: a Prayer for Guidance.**   Deut. 9. 25–29.
   Hymn 91, "Guide me, O thou great Jehovah."

4. **The Cloud by Day: the Fire by Night.**   Exod. 13. 20–22.
   Hymn 95, "When Israel of the Lord beloved."

5. **The Voice of God.**   Exod. 20. 1–18.
   Hymn 211 (verses 1, 2), "Hear what God the Lord hath spoken."

6. **Onward through the Wilderness.**   Deut. 1. 5–11.
   Hymn 567, "Through the night of doubt and sorrow."

7. **Moses' Vision from the Mountain.**   Deut. 34. 1–6.
   Hymn 604, "There is a land of pure delight."

8. **Marching Song.**   Josh. 1. 10–16.
   Hymn 384 (1st and last verses), "Forward be our watchword."

9. **At the River.**   Josh. 3. 7–13.
   Hymn 617 (1st, 2d, and last verses), "On Jordan's stormy banks I stand."

10. **The Battle.**   Josh. 6. 12–21.
    Hymn 448, "God is my strong salvation."

11. **Possession of the Promised Land.**   Josh. 18. 3–10.
    Hymn 403, "Defend us, Lord."   (Tune "Joshua.")

12. **Victory through Divine Power.**   Psa. 48. 1–14.
    Hymn 212, "Zion stands with hills surrounded."

Topic for Discussion: "What was the most Significant Event between Egypt and the Jordan?"

12. The Prophets and Prophecies

1. The Music of the Prophets.   Psa. 95. 1–6.
     Hymn 12 (verses 1, 3, 5), "O Thou, to whom in ancient
         time."

2. The Inspiration of Prophecy.   1 Pet. 1. 3–12.
     Hymn 181 (verses 1, 2), "Come, Holy Ghost, our
         hearts inspire."

3. The Pathway of the Prophets.   Heb. 11. 32–40.
     Hymn 306 (verses 1, 2), "Jesus, my all, to heaven
         is gone."

4. Prophecy Concerning the Coming of Christ.   Isa. 9. 1–7.
     Hymn 108 (verses 1, 5), "Hark, the glad sound! the
                                    Saviour comes,
                                The Saviour promised
                                    long."

5. Prophecy Concerning the Cross.   Isa. 53. 3–10.
     Hymn 149 (verses 2, 3), " 'Tis finished! all that heaven
                                    foretold
                                By prophets in the days of
                                    old."

6. The Golden Age.   Psa. 72. 3–18.
     Hymn 110 (verse 5), "For lo! the days are hastening on
                                By prophet-bards foretold."

7. The Testimony of the Prophets.   Acts 2. 25–36.
     Hymn 293, "Art thou weary, art thou languid?"
         (Verses 1, 2, 6, 7.)

8. Thanks for Prophecy.   (Prayer.)
     Hymn 14 (verses 1, 2, 4), "To thee, Eternal Soul, be
                                    praise!
                                Who from of old to our
                                    own days
                                Through souls of saints
                                    and prophets, Lord,
                                Hast sent thy light, thy
                                    love, thy word."

Topic for Discussion: "Who was the Greatest Prophet?"

13. Missions and Messengers

Opening Hymn, 111, "Hark! the herald angels sing!"

1. The Call.   Acts 16. 6–10.
   Hymn 655, "From Greenland's icy mountains."

2. The Command.   Mark 16. 14–19.
   Hymn 634, "Tell it out among the heathen."

3. Prayer for Divine Guidance.   Acts 4. 24–33.
   Hymn 220, "Jesus, the truth and power divine,
        Send forth these messengers of thine."

4. Response by the Messengers.   Acts 10. 34–43.
   Hymn 219, "Lord of the living harvest."

5. Parting Charge to the Messengers.   John 20. 19–22.
   Hymn 640, "Go, ye messengers of God!"

6. The Field, the Inspiration to Work.   Psa. 2. 1–10.
   Hymn 654 (verses 2, 3, 4), "Behold how many thou-
        sands."

7. The Invitation.   Acts 2. 29–39.
   Hymn 259 (second tune), "Come, ye sinners."

8. The Penitence of the Nations.   Acts 2. 40–43.
   Hymn 653, "The morning light is breaking."

9. The Fire of Salvation.   Acts 2. 1–4.
   Hymn 643, "See, how great a flame aspires!"

10. The Signs of the Times.   Isa. 21. 6–12.
    Hymn 636, "Watchman, tell us of the night."

11. The Final Conquest Completed.   Rev. 22. 1–6.
    Hymn 631, "Jesus shall reign where'er the sun."

12. The Banner of Victory.   (Recessional.)
    Hymn 639 (verses 1, 3, 4, 6), "Fling out the banner!"

Topic for Discussion: "Our Duty toward Missions."

14. THE MOUNTAINS

Opening Hymn, 649 (verses 2, 3), "See how beauteous on the mountains."

1. HOREB—The Mountain of Covenant. Lev. 20. 22–26.
   Hymn 403, "Defend us, Lord, from every ill."

2. PISGAH—The Mountain of Vision. Deut. 34. 1–6.
   Hymn 516 (verses 1, 3), "Sweet hour of prayer."

3. HATTIN—The Mountain of the Beatitudes. Matt. 5. 1–16.
   Hymn 360, "Blest are the pure in heart."

4. HERMON—The Mountain of Transfiguration. Mark 9. 2–10.
   Hymn 131, "O Master, it is good to be
   High on the mountain here with thee."

5. OLIVES—The Mountain of Anguish. Luke 22. 39–48.
   Hymn 147, " 'Tis midnight; and on Olive's brow."

6. CALVARY—The Mountain of Crucifixion. Luke 23. 32–47.
   Hymn 152, "O come and mourn with me awhile."

7. OLIVET—The Mountain of Ascension. Luke 24. 45–53.
   Hymn 162, "Hail the day that sees him rise."

Closing Hymn, 423 (verses 5, 6), "O Master, from the mountain side."

Topic for Discussion: "The Mountain-tops of Christian Experience."

15. THE SEA

1. Prayer for Those at Sea.   Psa. 107. 21–31.
   Hymn 59 (verses 1, 3), "Now the day is over."

2. The Sinful Soul on Life's Ocean.   Isa. 57. 15–21.
   Hymn 246 (verses 1, 2), "Sinners, the voice of God regard."

3. Christ in the Storm.   Matt. 8. 18–27.
   Hymn 485, "Fierce raged the tempest o'er the deep."

4. Jesus Walking on the Waves.   Matt. 14. 22–33.
   Hymn 61 (verses 1, 3), "The day is gently sinking to a close."

5. A Voice Divine Across the Waves.   John 21. 3–9, 15–19.
   Hymn 545, "Jesus calls us o'er the tumult."

6. "Pilot Me!"   Psa. 48. 7–14.
   Hymn 482, "Jesus, Saviour, pilot me."

7. Safe to the Land!   Isa. 33. 17–21; Ezek. 27. 29.
   Hymn 451, "My bark is wafted to the strand."

8. The Ocean of God's Love.   Psa. 107. 1–8.
   Hymn 98, "There's a wideness in God's mercy
   Like the wideness of the sea."

Topic for Discussion: "The Most Significant Sea Episode in the Bible."

16. Children's Day Service

Processional: Hymn 383, "Onward, Christian soldiers."

1. The Children of Israel in the Desert.   Exod. 40. 32–38.
   Hymn 681, "Brightly gleams our banner."

2. The Child in the Temple.   Sam. 3. 3–18.
   Hymn 674, "Hushed was the evening hymn."

3. The Christ Child.   Luke 2. 40–52.
   Hymn 678 (verses 5 and 6, or the whole hymn), "O Thou whose infant feet were found."

4. The Child in Jesus' Arms.   Mark 10. 13–16.
   Hymn 682, "I think when I read that sweet story of old."

5. The Child on Palm Sunday.   Mark 11. 1–11.
   Hymn 684, "There was a time, when children sang."

6. The Child in the Early Christian Church.   Eph. 6. 1–3, 14–17.
   Hymn 672, "Shepherd of tender youth."
   (The oldest Christian hymn extant, by Clement, A. D. 170–220.)

7. The Offerings of the Child.   (Collection for Christian Education.)
   Hymn 673, "Beauteous are the flowers of earth."

8. Prayer.
   Hymn 677, "Saviour, like a shepherd lead us."

9. Recessional.
   Hymn 680, "There's a Friend for little children."

17. SOLDIERS OF THE CROSS

1. The Call for Volunteers. Matt. 16. 24–27.
   Hymn 416, "The Son of God goes forth to war."

2. The Response. Isa. 6. 5–12.
   Hymn 393 (verses 1, 4, 5), "Am I a soldier of the cross?"

3. Swearing Allegiance. 2 Chron. 15. 10–15.
   Hymn 413 (verses 1, 2, 3), "Stand, soldier of the cross."

4. The Armor. Eph. 6. 11–18.
   Hymn 397 (verses 1, 2, 3), "Behold, the Christian warrior stands!"

5. The Call to Arms. Judg. 6. 13–16.
   Hymn 386, "Stand up! stand up for Jesus!"

6. Prayer to God for Defense. 2 Kings 19. 14–19.
   Hymn 403 (verses 1, 2), "Defend us, Lord, from every ill."

7. The Captain. Heb. 2. 5–10.
   Hymn 408, "Lead on! O King eternal!"

8. The Watchword. Judg. 12. 4–6 (*Shibboleth*).
   Hymn 420 (verses 1, 2), " True-hearted, whole-hearted."

9. Forward into Battle. Judg. 8. 16–22.
   Hymn 383 (verses 1, 2, 3), "Onward, Christian soldiers."

10. The Fight. 1 Tim. 6. 11–16.
    Hymn 409 (verses 1, 4), "Fight the good fight."

11. The Victory. 1 Cor. 15. 52–58.
    Hymn 418 (verses 1, 2), "We march, we march to victory!"

18. The Soul's Progress

1. The Depths of Sin. Rom. 7. 18–24.
   Hymn 242 (1st verse), "Plunged in a gulf of dark
   despair."

2. Warning. Matt. 3. 7–12.
   Hymn 247, "Sinners, turn; why will ye die?"

3. Judgment and Retribution. Rom. 2. 3–9.
   Hymn 603, "The day of wrath, that dreadful day."

4. Conviction. Acts 16. 25–31.
   Hymn 267, "Depth of mercy! can there be?"

5. Invitation. Matt. 11. 25–30.
   Hymn 259, "Come, ye sinners, poor and needy."

6. Acceptance. Matt. 9. 1–8.
   Hymn 272, "Just as I am."

7. Faith. Heb. 11. 1–10.
   Hymn 301, "Arise, my soul, arise."

8. Witness of the Spirit. Acts 2. 1–4.
   Hymn 304, "I heard the voice of Jesus say" (1st
   two verses).

9. Aspiration. Psa. 42. 1–5.
   Hymn 317, "More love, O Christ, to thee."

10. Consecration. Isa. 6. 5–12.
    Hymn 348, "Take my life, and let it be consecrated."

11. Temptation. Matt. 4. 1–11.
    Hymn 493, "My soul, be on thy guard."

12. Activity. James 2. 14–26.
    Hymn 397, "Behold the Christian warrior."

13. Heaven. Rev. 22. 1–5.
    Hymn 623, "Rise, my soul."

APPENDIX

Bible-study and mission-study classes are becoming important factors in arousing an intelligent interest in the teachings and work of the church. But why should we not also develop Hymnal-Study Classes to kindle a more intelligent interest in our worship? The very subject of the study should prove fascinating to young and old, and with wise leadership such classes could be made a success in almost every church in Methodism.

For the guidance of leaders of Hymnal-Study Classes the following outline has been prepared, more for purposes of suggestion than for prescribing a hard-and-fast course of study. The scheme may be varied according to the abilities and interests of the class and its leader. In the topics for preparation, especial encouragement should be given to the student to select illustrations for each point first-hand from the Hymnal. Frequently, if possible, the class should sing the hymns—especially after they have been analyzed in respect to the particular theme of that week's lesson. This should familiarize the class with many new hymns, and also with the best methods of studying other new hymns yet unlearned.

Nor need the study be confined to Methodists. An interdenominational class may find this plan of study of value, if only the first lesson be modified or omitted. Should such classes prove to be successful, the writer would be interested to hear of the progress of the class. If, as is intended, this study awakens a deeper interest in the hymns and their music, the effort of organizing and conducting the class would be well worth while.

Lesson I. Hymnal History

Assignment for Reading: Part I, Chapters 1, 2, and 3.

Topics for Special Preparation:

1. The Eighteenth Century Hymnals.
2. The Official Methodist Episcopal Hymnals (North and South).
3. The Making of the Present Hymnal.

4. The Hymnal and Other Factors, hastening the Union of
   the two Methodist Episcopal Churches, North and
   South.

5. A Critique of Hymnals, Now Used in Other Denominations. (Examine the hymnals in other churches in
   your town.)

Lesson II.   Spiritual Conditions Producing Hymns

Assignment for Reading: Part II, Chapter 4, pp. 59–79.

Topics for Special Preparation:

1. Old Testament Hymns, of Moses, Hannah, David.
2. New Testament Hymns, of Mary, the Gloria in Excelsis,
   Revelation.
3. Sorrow-Inspired Hymns.
4. Joy-Inspired Hymns.
5. Hymns Celebrating Conversion from Sin.

Lesson III.   The Power of Hymns in Human Life

Assignment for Reading: Chapter 4, pp. 79–94.

Topics for Special Preparation:

1. New Hymn Stories (let the members of the Class ask
   several Christian people for their experiences with
   hymns).
2. The Effectiveness of Hymns in the Salvation of Souls.
3. Hymns at the Portal of Death.
4. War Songs.
5. The Different Ways in which Hymns are Used.

Lesson IV.   The Schools of Hymn-Writers in English

Assignment for Reading: Chapter 5, pp. 95–112.

Topics for Special Preparation:

1. Famous Literary Folk who were Hymn-Writers.
2. The Eighteenth Century Hymn-Writers.
3. The Oxford Movement and Hymnody and the Wesleyan
   Movement.
4. Clergymen as Hymn-Writers.
5. Hymn-Writing in America.

Lesson V.   Hymns in Foreign Languages

Assignment for Reading: Chapter 5, pp. 112–128.

Topics for Special Preparation:
1. The Greek Hymnists.
2. Hymns from the Latin Church.
3. Wesley's Translations from the German.
4. Hymns from the Hebrew Scriptures.
5. Missionary Hymns.

Lesson VI.   Theological Teaching in the Hymns

Assignment for Reading: Chapter 6.

Topics for Special Preparation:
1. The Hymns as Teachers of Theology.
2. What Hymns Can the Roman Catholics Use from Our Hymnal?
3. What Hymns Can the Unitarians Use from Our Hymnal?
4. Which of Our Hymns are Common to All Christians?
5. Which of Our Hymns are Peculiar to Methodism?

Lesson VII.   The Literary Beauties of the Hymns

Assignment for Reading: Chapter 7.

Topics for Special Preparation:
1. Emotions Expressed in the Hymns (with illustrations).
2. Subjective and Objective Hymns.
3. The Imagery in the Hymns.
4. Literary Blemishes in the Hymns of Other Hymnals.
5. The Rhythm of the Hymns.

Lesson VIII.   The Contribution of Each Nation to the Tunes of the Hymnal

Assignment for Reading: Chapter 8.

Topics for Special Preparation:
1. Music as a Universal Language.
2. Hymn-Tune Composers from the Continent of Europe.
3. Hymn-Tune Composers from Great Britain.
4. American Hymn-Tune Composers.

5. Larger Compositions from which Hymn-Tunes are Derived. (Under this heading it would add interest if some musician would render some of the larger sources of hymn-tunes.)   See page 263.

LESSON IX.   STORIES OF THE TUNES AND THEIR TITLES

Assignment for Reading: Chapter 9 and a Review of Chapter 8.

Topics for Special Preparation:

1. How Tunes are Composed (see text).
2. What are the Best Tunes?
3. Different Reasons for Choosing Tune-Titles.
4. National and Patriotic Tunes in the Hymnal.
5. Secular Songs that have Made Hymn-Tunes.

LESSON X.   INTERPRETATION OF THE HYMNS THROUGH THE MUSIC

Assignment for Reading: Chapter 10.

Topics for Special Preparation:

1. Should Hymn-Tunes be Emotional, and Why?
2. What Hymn-Tunes Best Describe the Emotions of Words?
3. Examples of Emotional Incongruity between Hymns and Words.
4. Should Music be Employed to Describe Events or Episodes.
5. A Study of Hymns 250–275, and their Relative Emotional Powers.

LESSON XI.   FORMAL ELEMENTS OF MUSIC

Assignment for Reading: Chapter 11.

Topics for Special Preparation:

1. The Value of Tunes with a Chorus.
2. What is the Purpose of Form in Music?
3. Which Keys are Best Suited to Hymn-Tunes?
4. What Elements of Form are Illustrated in the Hymn-Tunes?
5. Find Illustrations of Poor Forms.

LESSON XII.   REVIEW AND PRACTICAL APPLICATION OF THE COURSE

Assignment for Reading: Chapter 12.
General Review.

INDEX

Lines in quotation are first lines of hymns. Lines in italics are titles of tunes.

"A mighty fortress is our God," 122, 254 (see "Ein' Feste Burg")

"Abide with me," 68, 104, 184, 193, 194, 226

Adams, Mrs. Sarah F., 110, 111, 133

Addison, Joseph, 77, 97, 156, 226

Ahle, Johann Rudolf, 171

"Alas! and did my Saviour," 87, 88, 187

Aldrich, Henry, 176

Alexander, Mrs. C. F., 111, 125

Alexander, J. W., 120, 122

Alford, Dean Henry, 75, 104

"All glory, laud," 118

"All hail! the power," 89, 101

All Saints, 176

Alsace, 197

Alverson, J. B., 27

"Am I a soldier of the," 151

America, 48, 176, 200, 236, 240

Amsterdam, 177

"Ancient of days," 108

"And are we yet alive?" 82

"And can it be that I," 61

"Another six days' work," 102

Antioch, 172, 196

"Arise, my soul, arise," 86

Arlington, 176, 199

Armenia, 188

Arne, Thomas A., 176, 199

"Art thou weary, art thou," 117, 127, 159

"As pants the hart for," 114

Asbury, Bishop, 19, 20, 21

Ashford, Mrs. E. L., 195, 208

"Asleep in Jesus," 76, 223

Auber, Miss Harriet, 110

Austria, 187

"Author of faith," 127

Avison, 178

"Awake, our souls! away," 151

Babcock, Rev. Dr. M. D., 109

Baker, Rev. Sir H. W., 82, 105, 106, 183, 206

Barbauld, Mrs. Anna L., 110

Baring-Gould, Rev. S., 105, 113

Barnby, Sir J., 181, 190, 207, 211, 214, 222, 241

Barthélémon, F. H., 174

Bartholdy, 197

Bartlett, Dr. Maro L., 195

Bathurst, Rev. William H., 104

Baume, John W., 196, 211

Baxter, Richard, 67, 97

Beddome, Rev. Benjamin, 102

Beethoven, **173,** 197, 200, 228

"Before J e h o v a h's a w f u l throne," 89

"Behold! the Christian warrior," 99

"Behold the Saviour of mankind," 85, 100

Belleville, 193

Bentley, 185

Bernard of Clairvaux, 120, 122

Bernard of Cluny, 119

Bickersteth, Rev. Dr. Edward H., 105, 148, 158

Black, J. M., 36

Blacklock, Rev. Thomas, 70

"Blessed assurance," 70, 90, 205

"Blest are the pure," 103

"Blest be the dear uniting," 90

"Blest be the tie," 74, 102

Boardman, 189

Boehm, Anthony W., 122

Bonar, Dr. Horatius, 75, 104

287

"O worship the King," 103
"Of all the thoughts of God," 106
"Of Him, who did salvation bring," 122
Old Hundred, 173, 199, 200, 206, 242
Oldberg, Arne, 173
Oliver, Henry Kemble, 188
Olivers, Rev. Thomas, 101, 113, 252
Olmutz, 170
Olney, 174, 185, 198
"One more day's work for Jesus," 191
"One sweetly solemn thought," 69, 165, 224
"Onward, Christian soldiers!" 105, 182, 212, 224, 225
Ortonville, 188

Paisello, Giovanni, 186
Palmer, Rev. Dr. Ray, 66, 108, 120
Pass me not, 191
Parker, Rev. Dr. F. S., 37, 210
Parry, Sir Charles Hubert H., 185, 186, 228
Passion Chorale, 171, 199, 201
Patten, David, Jr., 27
Peace, A. L., 184
"Peace, perfect peace," 105, 227
Perronet, Rev. Edward, 102
Pleyel, Ignaz Joseph, 187, 198
Pleyel's Hymn, 187, 198, 227
Pond, Sylvester Billings, 188
Pontius, William H., 194
Portuguese Hymn, 202
"Praise God, from whom," 96
"Prayer is the soul's sincere," 99
Precious name, 191
Prentiss, Mrs. E. P., 111
Procter, Adelaide Ann, 111
Purcell, Thomas, 176, 185
Puritan, 193

Quayle, Bishop W. A., 31

Radiant Morn, 174, 206
Rankin, Rev. Dr. J. E., 109

Rathbun, 189
Redhead, R., 182, 215, 239
Redner, Lewis Henry, 192
"Rescue the perishing," 66, 191
Retreat, 188
"Return, O wanderer," 147
Rice, Mrs. Caroline Laura, 112
Richter, Rev. Dr. Christian F., 123
"Ride on, ride on in majesty," 104
Rinkart, Martin, 124
"Rise, glorious Conqueror," 104
"Rise, my soul, and stretch thy wings," 101
Ritter, Peter, 184
Robinson, Rev. Robert, 64, 102
"Rock of Ages," 82, 102, 127, 128
Rodigast, Samuel, 125
Rogers, Lebbeus Harding, 84
Roosevelt, Theodore, 209
Rossini, Gioachino A., 186
Rothe, Johann A., 123
Rotterdam, 187
Rousseau, Jean Jacques, 174, 198
Russian Hymn, 186, 201
Rutherford, 174, 211

St. Athanasius, 182
St. Andrew of Crete, 117, 220
St. Ann, 52, 176, 201
St. George's, Windsor, 182
St. John of Damascus, 117
St. John's, Westminster, 180
St. Leonard, 182
St. Louis, 192
St. Martin's, 177
St. Peter, 171, 201, 203
St. Petersburg, 186
St. Stephen, 177
St. Theodulph, 171
St. Theodulph of Orleans, 118
St. Theresa, 121
St. Thomas, 187
Samson, 197
Sanctus, No. 2, 194
Sankey, Ira D., 191
"Saviour, again to thy dear," 75, 105, 229

DATE DUE

MAR 2 2 1985			